This book is aimed at Parish Councillor  to provide some guidance and wisdom of law, on Defamation, freedom of sp to know. (including full legal cases)

I am particularly grateful to the late Tom Toward, Town Clerk of Shildon Town Council, the late Councillor Walter Nunn also of Shildon Town Council, the Late Councillor Eric White and of course Councillor Bob Fleming Leader of Great Aycliffe Town Council. I had the honour of proposing both Eric and Bob for the position of Honorary Freemen both having served over 30 years as Councillors. I have known these people from the age of 16 when I went into politics and they have inspired me by their wisdom, knowledge, integrity and above all….. humility.   Men of great virtue who had done many noble deeds.

My thanks also to Andrew Bailey our Town Clerk on Great Aycliffe Town Council for giving this book a once over and keeping me right. Andrew has been with our Council almost 30 years. As Town Clerk he has been totally impartial, taken the rough with the smooth and set a high standard. He is a fine example of what a Town Clerk should be.

I hope this book proves useful as a guide to knowledgeable amateurs everywhere.   I remember once when fighting the old guard in politics one said to me "a little knowledge is dangerous" to which I replied" show me the person who has so much knowledge as to be out of danger"

We never stop learning.

Councillor Arun M Chandran

Some people are born chairmen. They have exactly the right temperament for the office and they know just how to proceed in any circumstance. But many are not so favourably gifted; yet it often happens that those who are less favoured may possess some peculiar knowledge which makes it imperative that they should take up the office. Accordingly, it is not at all rare to find a man or woman seated in the chair who feels very much out of place in that important position.

As this is written primarily for the individual who allows himself to be elected to the chair more as a sense of duty than from a love of power, we will begin by supposing that you have attended a meeting and, somewhat to your surprise, you find that it is the will of those present that you should take the chair.
Probably, your first inclinations will be to reject the honour which the meeting wishes to confer on you, and you will set about hiding your light under a bushel. This is a very natural attitude on your part, and it speaks, well for your modesty; but it is not a line of action in which you should persist. After the first shock of finding yourself in the centre of the limelight, your duty is to pull yourself together and accept the honour graciously. After all, every chairman, even the most gifted, had to make a start at some time or other and, unless you belong to the very nervous type of person, there is no reason at all why you should not make a complete success of the office when you have once thrown yourself into the work.

The necessary qualities of a chairman:

The primary duty of a chairman is to control and guide the meeting. Where a number of people are gathered together, it is only reasonable to suppose that many divergent views will exist. Some will want one thing, some another. Some will express themselves in a friendly manner; others will become heated and aggressive.

No matter what the situation, the chairman must remain placid throughout, and hold the scales fairly between the various parties. Above all, he must be firm and show no weakness. This should not be interpreted to mean, however, that the chairman has the right to brow-beat or bully those who speak. Actually, bullying is a sign of weakness; it shows that the chairman is uncertain of his own powers and that he adopts extreme measures in order to cloak his deficiencies.

In many ways the chairman of a meeting is like the referee at a football match, and one indispensable qualification is impartiality. It would be hypocritical to say that he must always feel impartial, for if he is an ordinary intelligent human being he will certainly have views, sometimes strong ones, on matters that are argued under his chairmanship. Impartiality means keeping his views to himself. This doesn't mean only that he must not air them: he must exercise himself to prevent the meeting from inferring what they are. Except on points of procedure the chairman should never seek to express his opinions unless he is specifically asked to do so by the meeting or by his Group. Nor should he ever try to guide the meeting towards a particular decision, or in any way influence its consideration of the point at issue unless it is his group's policy. In particular he must not show any favouritism towards speakers with whose opinions he is in sympathy, or hostility towards those with whom he personally disagrees.

The Leader and Deputy Leader should normally be looked upon to provide a lead or help close a debate. They have no legal standing at Parish level, and the Proposers and seconders rights always come first in accordance with Standing Orders.

Normally every speaker must address his remarks to the Chair. Only one person at a time is allowed to speak, and one of the Chairman's tasks is to see that this rule is kept. If two or more persons try to speak at the same time he should decide which should speak first. Sometimes an agreed rotation of speakers will have been decided beforehand, but more commonly, after a motion has been proposed and seconded, the right to speak next goes to whoever is the first to raise their hand. A chairman is not compelled to give any member a hearing, but if he seems to be deliberately excluding anyone, perhaps to favour someone else, he can be overruled by the carrying of a motion " that Cllr. — be heard." if such a motion is proposed and seconded, the chairman is bound to put the question to the meeting without further debate, and if it is carried he must enforce it. But this is exceptional, for it can only occur when the chairman is trying to thwart the will of much of the meeting.

The chairman must know the rules. He should have a thorough grasp of meeting procedure in general and of the particular rules or Standing Orders of the body that has met. Like the referee at a football match, again, he should know the rules better than anyone else there. He will lose all respect and therefore authority if, for example, he is caught out on a point of order.

Knowledge of the rules is necessary but should not be flaunted.

The best referee is not the one who blows the whistle most frequently, and the chairman must try to keep the meeting going with as few interruptions by himself as he can. He must certainly see that the rules are obeyed, but he should interpret them broadly, according to the spirit rather than in a narrowly legalistic literal sense.

The worst qualification for a chairman is fondness of the sound of one's own voice. Chairmen should be more seen than heard. They should not speak at all unless they need to, and then they should be very brief.
One of the difficulties of chairmanship is the fact that often it is impracticable for everyone to address the meeting for as long as he likes. It may be impossible through lack of time, or undesirable because some speakers are long-winded and stray a way from the subject under discussion. Curbing such speakers in the interests of

the meeting in general calls for considerable tact. It is not always easy to decide whether the speaker has introduced irrelevant matters —when challenged he usually shows honest surprise-- and the chairman should not interfere unless he thinks there is no other way of bringing the speaker back to the matter in hand. The chairman should be very, very reluctant to use his power, after warning the speaker, to order him to stop speaking. Hurt pride rouses feelings of grievance, and after such action there is usually at least one member of the meeting who has lost confidence in the chairman's impartiality. For this reason it is often a good thing to have a general time-limit on all speeches. (usually in Standing Orders).

The chairman does not have to enforce this to the second, but if speakers need to be curbed this automatic mechanical brake is likely to arouse less resentment than a personal order from the chair.

While the chairman should in general be tactful, courteous, and benign, never bossy or school masterish, he must also show that when necessary he can be firm. While he should do as little as possible himself to impede the orderly flow of the meeting, he must not tolerate interruptions by anyone else. He can—and should—still be courteous, but he must not be weak or timid in calling to order persons who interrupt a speaker or whisper audibly during a speech. The only permitted interruption is on a point of order, when another member may rise and raise a specific point. The chairman must decide on the point quickly and definitely, without allowing any debate or discussion. Having decided, he must stand by his decision. If he shows-any weakness or half-heartedness he will lose respect for the chair.
This respect is vital if order is to be kept. Except when it can lie supported by physical threats -as, for example, in schools or prisons or Her Majesty's Forces —discipline depends on voluntary submission to authority, and that is only granted when the authority is regarded with general respect.

Thus it all come to this: A chairman must allow all sides to voice their opinions; he must be fair to all: he must have no opinions of his own if the harmony of the meeting is likely to be endangered by their expression: he must be genially disposed to all sides: and he must see to it that there is no wavering from the real business in hand.

AN OUTLINE OF THE CHAIRMAN'S DUTIES:

So far, we have dealt with the chairman's duties in a general way. Now we will explain how a meeting should be conducted. At every meeting the chairman has definite duties to perform. If he is new to the work, it will be a good idea to write the items on a slip of paper and have them in front of him while the meeting is proceeding.

There will then be no fear of missing any vital point. Always have some paper and pen with you and write people's names down as the indicate they wish to speak, that way they know they caught your eye, and don't have to keep putting their hands up to be next, and will be called in turn, and you know the order in which to call people to speak, and can pay more attention to what people are saying.

They are:

(i) To make sure that the meeting has been convened correctly. In most cases there will be no doubt about this. The summons paper states the time, place and other particulars. These will, of course, be adhered to. For instance, it would be unpardonable to start ten minutes early.

The chairman must satisfy himself that the proper notice has been given. As a matter of fact, he will do this before the meeting.

There is no need to read the Agenda Item out word for word; everyone has it in front of them. Likewise Reports by Officers, the Chairman should ask the if relevant Officer has anything he/she wants to add or explain in their report otherwise every member will have had time to read and study it so it does not need the Officer to go through it line by line !

(ii) To see that a quorum is present. Full Council one third of members. Committees and Sub-Committees 3 members.

In the Standing Orders, rules, etc., of a body, it is invariably laid down that a certain minimum number of persons are required to be present at a meeting to make the meeting valid. When the minimum number is present, a quorum is formed and the meeting can proceed. It is the chairman's duty to see that this point is observed.

(iii) To state the purpose of the meeting.

The chairman opens the meeting by stating its purpose, as each member has received a copy the chairman merely refers to it and announces that the meeting will proceed to deal with the first item. This is usually the minutes of the last meeting. Apologies (as per sheet) should be given before the meeting or after, and reading out the public notice of the meeting word for word is totally unnecessary.

(iv) To have the minutes read of the previous meeting. Indicated by a show of hands, the Town Clerk will ask for a proposer and seconder. No motion or discussion of the minutes is allowed before they are confirmed, except in regard to their literal accuracy. After they have been confirmed, however, members of the meeting may ask questions or make comments on any matters arising out of them. This, indeed, is usually the second item on the agenda paper, and in that case the chairman asks the meeting if anyone has any questions or comments. On Councils matters arising are usually in reports or separate agenda items.

(v) To proceed with as much of the business set down on the agenda as time allows.

This, of course, is the real work that the meeting has been called to perform. It may begin with the chairman's or Officer's report, and then perhaps other reports.

Then there may be motions and perhaps amendments; votes of thanks; and, finally the chairman declares the meeting closed.

DISTURBANCES:

There is no doubt that the Englishman's love of fair play is such that at most meetings the chairman has little difficulty, if he possesses tact, in keeping order. But although he will seldom need to fall back on stern measures, it is highly important that he should know how to act when disorder does occur.

The Public Meeting Act, 1908, provides that any person at a lawful public meeting who acts in a disorderly manner for the purpose of preventing the transaction of the business for which the meeting was called is guilty of an offence, and on conviction is liable to a fine not exceeding £5 or imprisonment not exceeding one month.

The Public Order Act, 1936, provides that any person at a public meeting who uses threatening, abusive, or insulting words or behaviour with intent to provoke a breach of the peace, or whereby a breach of the peace is likely to be caused, is guilty of an offence, and on conviction is liable to imprisonment not exceeding three months or to a fine not exceeding £50 or to both imprisonment and fine. A constable without warrant may arrest any person whom he reasonably suspects of committing an offence under the 1936 Act.
Further, he may, if asked by the chairman of the meeting, require such a person to declare to him immediately his name and address, and if the person refuses he is guilty of an offence and is liable on conviction to a fine not exceeding forty shillings.

I remember at a Committee meeting many years ago, the Chairman after several attempts to resolve a situation had to adjourn the meeting and the police were called and subsequently escorted two Councillors from the Chamber, whereupon the meeting continued.

It is rare, however, that the law will need to be invoked. But it is there if needed. Usually, the utmost which a chairman will feel disposed to do is to declare the meeting closed and, when he has left the chair, all further discussion is without value.

Or he can adjourn the meeting for a definite period of time. This is usually the better plan, as to close the meeting sacrifices the whole of the occasion. An adjournment for, say, fifteen minutes loses no more time than is needed to enable the disorderly element to come to its senses.

A POINT OF ORDER:

It is very clear that occasions may arise when the person who is speaking permits himself to make some offensive remark. The remark may consist of insulting or improper language, or one of a thousand other things. Generally, the chairman will immediately interfere; but it is clear that the remark may be of such a character that the chairman is not to know of its derogatory nature. When this occurs, it is open to anyone in the meeting to rise and interrupt the speaker. He uses the formula, "Mr. Chairman, I rise on a point of order." He does not wait for the speaker to finish his speech and he need not wait for a pause in his words; he simply talks louder than the one who has made the offensive remark. The original speaker must give way to allow the interrupter to say what the point of order is, and the chairman then has to decide whether or not the interrupter was correct in drawing his attention to it. If a remark is considered offensive the speaker is normally required to withdraw it.   Standing Orders empower a Chairman to name a Councillor and that Councillor must cease forthwith....   Know your Standing Orders.

If a member notices an irregularity or error in procedure that has escaped the attention of the chairman —for example, if there is not a quorum or if the wording of a motion is faulty—he may similarly interrupt on a point of order. Similar action may be taken by any member if, for example, whispering is going on and the chairman is not using his authority to stop it.

DEBATES AND PROCEDURE:

The chairman must know the rules of debate. His duty is to enforce them. Speakers must know the rules either to follow them or to attempt to evade them.

The chairman is in charge. He has been elected or appointed to his position and is expected to guide and control the meeting. He is in charge of proceedings. When the chairman stands, everyone else is expected to sit and to be silent. If the chairman cannot obtain order by rapping his gavel and demanding silence, he may have to adjourn the meeting. Unless the meeting is closed, the chairman is entitled to speak whenever he wishes—and to prevent anyone else from doing so unless he wishes. He decides the order of speeches. He will have the agenda but may vary it   He is in charge.
But, of course, he should rule by consent. For instance, if he decides to change the order of business, he should explain his reasons. If the bulk of the meeting objects to the change, then he should normally revert to the original order. He is not a dictator.

Normally, each item of business should be discussed separately. If there are steps to be taken—or even if it is to be resolved that there be no action on the matter—a resolution or motion will be 'put'. This can be done quite informally, where there is either no opposition or a general consensus. But if after discussion has taken place there is no agreement, there should be a vote where the formalities are being observed, a motion will be proposed and seconded.

It will then be thrown open to the meeting for discussion- and the chairman will attempt to call upon someone who will oppose the motion. After the matter has been sufficiently ventilated, the proposer will normally exercise his right of reply. Then a vote may have to be taken.

If the motion or resolution is not on the agenda, the proposer should be asked to phrase it as concisely and clearly as possible. The chairman who has to put a resolution which even the proposer has not put into sensible English (and into words which can be put into the minute book) is in a bad way. The motion should be clearly stated either by the proposer or by the chairman before it goes forward for debate.

The length and number of speeches will depend upon the chairman. But anyone may 'move the closure'. Or it may be resolved that 'the question be now put. A show of hands will indicate whether those present have had enough of the subject or whether they wish to debate the matter further. If a chairman is in doubt as to whether or not the debate should be closed— or if he feels that it would appear partisan for him to terminate it—then he can easily test the feeling of the meeting, if necessary by asking whether anyone wishes 'to move the closure'.

If it is agreed that the question 'be now put—then that is what happens. The motion is voted upon. If a motion is carried that the meeting move on-to 'next business', then no vote is taken on the motion. It is often better not to reveal the split in the ranks. Or all sides may prefer to avoid a vote which no one is really confident of winning.

The effect of this being passed is that the discussion on the current topic terminates. No vote is, of course, taken on the matter in question.

There are times when people feel that it would have been better for the organization or meeting had the discussion not taken place at all.

Again, someone may move that the entire meeting be adjourned. It is not only the chairman who can terminate the proceedings. If those present at the meeting wish to put an end to it, they may normally do so. But, of course, there may be a lengthy debate 'on the adjournment'. Whilst the debate goes on, there may be interruptions

One common device is a 'point of order'. Anyone is entitled to raise any point he wishes concerning the order of the meeting, at any time. In theory, he is only free to query as to whether the procedure in hand ... what the speaker is saying . . . the chairman's ruling ... is 'in order'. He should not stray away to deal with side issues or to use the occasion to deal with the substantive issues. But skilled interrupters can often disguise their disruptive attacks in the form of 'points of order', and so insinuate extra speeches where none would otherwise be allowed. In some meetings, the custom is for speakers to give way on 'points of information'—but generally, it is a matter for them (the speakers themselves) to decide.

The chairman cannot force them to give way, or take any step if they decline to do so. But if the chairman himself addresses the speaker, the latter may remain speaking but (like anyone else at the meeting) must accord the chairman the right to speak—and whilst he does so, must remain silent.
The speaker, then, must 'obey the chairman's ruling'. The fact that he 'has the floor' does not mean that he is entitled to occupy it in the teeth of objection from the chair.

If all motions were proposed, seconded, opposed and voted upon as they stood, a chairman's life would be moderately easy.

But there are always amendments to be considered.

In general, motions to amend a resolution must (if seconded) be allowed. They should be considered individually and voted upon if necessary. If accepted (whether or not after a vote) they become incorporated into the original motion, which must then be put, as amended. If rejected, they die. An amended motion, once put, can then be the subject of further amendment, with the procedure as before.

Often a skilled chairman can manage to induce the mover of a resolution to vary or extend its terms so as to incorporate the amendment. A peaceful meeting is a chairman's delight. But equally, if an amendment is really no more than an attempt to kill the resolution, he may rule it out of order and require the proposer of the amendment to put forward his views in opposition to the substantive motion. The chairman's job is to ensure that everyone is given a reasonable opportunity to express his views. But he is not bound to allow a minority to dominate. He is entitled not only to select the speakers (in the fairest possible way), but also to sort out the resolutions and the amendments, so that the feelings of the meeting may be tested in the fairest way.

Note, then, that once the meeting has a reasonable opportunity to express its view, the chairman himself may with the consent of the meeting—close the debate and put the motion to the vote.

Some additional points:

No one has any right to speak more than once on any motion or amendment—although the proposer of an original motion (but not usually of an amendment) will generally be given the right to reply. Leaders and Deputy Leaders of political groups have no legal standing.

Once a motion has been defeated, it should not be allowed back into the meeting under some other guise.

No amendment can be proposed after the original motion has been passed or rejected.

Amendments cannot be proposed or seconded by those who performed that service for the original motion; but they can, of course, accept (or speak on) the amendments proposed by others.

If you wish to frame an amendment, the best way is usually to do so by moving that the words you have in mind be added to or omitted from or inserted into (as the case may be) the motion or resolution.

Meetings are usually governed by consent and common sense. The chairman must keep his head and never panic. Speakers should help the chair in every case except that in which the chairman has shown himself "to be unwilling to act impartially. In that case, the battle is on.

MOTIONS:

Usually any member may propose a motion but it cannot be debated or voted on unless it has a seconder apart from motions from the chair which need no seconder. Priority should be given to written motions sent in advance and appearing on the agenda together with names of proposer and seconder. All motions, written or verbal should be clearly read out by the chairman

It is then the proposer's privilege to 'Speak to the Motion and the seconder may follow immediately or reserve the right to speak later after some discussion has ensued. Speeches in opposition should be given just as much time as the supporters' contributions but to avoid unduly lengthy discussion and repetition the chairman is in order to request brevity and may see fit to impose time limits.

He should of course endeavour to be scrupulously fair between the rival factions, especially when closing the discussion to take a vote and exercising his privilege to sum up if he thinks there is any confusion.

It is open to other members, who feel that the discussion has gone on long enough, to take action. A member may move that 'The motion be now put'. The chairman must ask if there is a seconder and providing there is then he must ask for a show of hands. A majority vote on this point obliges the chairman to put the motion to the vote without further debate but before allowing this to arise he should be sure the principals had had their say and draw attention for instance to a seconder not having been given his reserved rights.

Once a motion has been voted on and passed by a requisite majority it becomes a Resolution which is binding and cannot be amended so we must next deal with amendments before we go on to methods of voting.

AMENDMENTS:

Any motion can be stopped before the vote is taken by a member proposing an amendment, which must be duly seconded, and a discussion will usually ensue followed by a vote on the amendment. If it be passed then the motion should be read out with the amendment incorporated and voted on in that form. Would that that were the whole story but life is not that simple. As often as not there will be other amendments, each separately debated and then incorporated or rejected as the voting may require. But worse is to come. There can be an amendment to an amendment before the original amendment is voted on and the last must be settled first and work back in that order. It can be very difficult to keep track and the final vote must be on the original Motion as amended.

The chairman has to watch for amendments that are really alter-native motions. They must not be accepted as amendments though the substance thereof may well enter into the discussions and those who prefer an alternative proposal should endeavour to gain their end by voting against the motion (amended or otherwise) and, if it be rejected, introduce the new motion.

Two more points remain on amendments. One is that there is no objection to the apparent contradiction of voting for an amendment when you are opposed to the whole motion because you may very well feel that second best to throwing out a motion you find unacceptable may be suffering only a less unacceptable amended version. It is a precautionary measure prior to trying to get all your own way.

The other point is that the proposer of a motion who senses that the members are against him may elect to save further trouble and perhaps acrimonious discussion by simply asking leave to withdraw the motion. This can be permitted at the chairman's discretion subject only to the assent of the seconder and may be wholly disallowed if the members feel that it should be put to the vote for any reason at all. One reason might be that supporters felt the proposer had 'cold feet' and could have gone on to win, and another might be that a clear majority vote against the motion might insure against it being brought up again at the first convenient occasion. Once in the minutes as a rejected motion it would not be permitted on the agenda again unless the circumstances had altered.

VOTING:

This is not as simple as might be supposed. It can be quite simple, especially at a small meeting, but it is necessary to know the variations.
It is usual to take a show of hands in the first place and if it is overwhelmingly one way it is acceptable. Any doubt should be removed by a count and perhaps a recount if close but there are circumstances in which a show of hands is inadequate. A named vote may be called to clarify the numbers and eligibility of those voting.

But always remember, and remind people if necessary, that in law an abstention is counted as for.   Or for political reasons you want proof of who voted for or against.   Or to be bloody minded if you want to use delaying tactics.

There may be abstainers in which case the verdict is 'nem con' which means 'none against' and this is not the same thing at all. An abstainer may raise a protest if his deliberate abstention is ignored.

CASTING VOTE:

There is often controversy on the matter of the customary right of a chairman to settle an equal vote by exercising his right to record a casting vote. This is open to more than one meaning and a chairman should make quite sure he knows his rights before applying them. On the Council he is to have a normal vote as a member with an additional deciding vote to employ when and if the figures equal out.

There is, however, no obligation to use the casting vote at all and unless the issue has to be settled one way or the other as a matter of urgency the wiser course is usually not to use the privilege. An equal vote means a strong division of opinion which may resolve itself in time and cause less dissension when members have had more time to think about it and the stronger views have cooled off a bit. A 'dead heat' automatically carries the item forward to the next meeting and often achieves this end; There remains only the matter of passing motions without taking a vote. (This is not a misprint — I do mean "no vote.) A chairman should at all times sense the feeling of the meeting and on minor issues on which it is perfectly clear that there is complete unison it is entirely superfluous to waste time counting.

A chairman would in such circumstances say something like 'We seem to be of one mind. Shall I take it that you wish me to record this motion as passed (or rejected)?'
General cries of assent will be deemed sufficient to record the passage of the motion in the minutes. Any member may of course insist on a vote being taken. There is no secret voting by Councils that is unlawful.

when others 'carry on'

POINTS OF ORDER:

At any meeting and at any time a member may stand up and say "Mr Chairman, on a point of order" and the chairman is under an obligation to take his point as a matter of priority.

It is hardly surprising that this rule is open to convenient misunderstanding by those who wish to interrupt in their own interests so it must be fully understood by all chairmen. A point of order means exactly what it says and concerns procedure and not the subject matter.

A permissible point of order might be that the person speaking at the time was in fact, for some reason within the rules, not entitled to speak at all. Another reason might be that the meeting had a time limit which had been exceeded. Whatever it may be, it must concern the conduct of the meeting and not be used to get in extra opinion on the debate.

Chairmen be warned. You will be lucky indeed if no one ever tries it on and the most usual and sometimes very subtle way of doing it is to challenge a statement by the person speaking. For example, "On a point of order, Mr Chairman, the population of this country is not a hundred million, it is only about half that figure," That was not a point of order at all.

It was point of fact and entirely out of order. Watch it! A persistent offender should be openly reprimanded and disallowed further participation in the discussions. A genuine point of procedure raised at the right time may, on the other hand, save a lengthy discussion on something outside the scope of the meeting which the chairman had inadvertently allowed to be brought up.

A wide-awake member might remember that the topic under discussion had already been left to a sub-committee to investigate and further mention pending their report was out of order and time-wasting.

Interruptions

Subtle pseudo-points of order are by no means the only unauthorised punctuations to the procedure. There are variations on the theme from calling out a quick word or two to shouting a speaker down, and others may join in.

Tolerating offenders

This is not a noble act of leniency it is surrender to a noisy minority at the expense of all else present. The majority will be solidly behind you if you find yourself in one of these uncomfortable chairs (not called 'the hot seat' without reason) and you assert your authority and refuse to let the meeting continue until interrupters have subsided. Probably the most difficult task of all is to be firm with offenders well-known to you and senior to you, perhaps, but have no fear. I have never heard a chairman criticized for being strong whereas sloppy chairmen are seldom invited to fulfil the role again. Keep your temper, be firm but not rude and the first interruption of the meeting will probably be the last.

Heckling

This must have some brief separate mention because there is a very big difference between trying to get a point of view in out of turn and trying to wreck a meeting. Some hecklers do not actually say anything but just shout or otherwise make a noise by way of protest. This is more or less limited to political meetings with highly controversial issues under discussion.

Ejection should be a last resort and the mere threat of it will silence all but the brave. When any meeting becomes overheated and tempers are rising a very good way to get calm is to adjourn rather than close down. Call a break for ten minutes and some of the mutual valedictions may get ironed out over a cup of tea or a stroll down the corridor.

Emergencies

Talking of maintaining calm, in the event of fire, accident, or any other unpredictable possible cause of panic the chairman is captain of the ship and should keep his position on the bridge and endeavour to direct, a display of calm from the chair being more likely to mitigate the trouble than anything else.

At all times while a meeting is in session the chair should not be vacated and a chairman who is obliged to leave the platform (to take an urgent telephone call for example) should put someone else in that seat until he gets back. There is always somebody in charge on the bridge.

ANY OTHER BUSINESS:

In case you did not know, it is unlawful for a Council to make a decision under "Any other business" so there is no any other business!   (but urgent information can be imparted)

Case Law states that a council cannot lawfully decide any matter which is not specified in the summons: **(Longfield Parish Council versus Wright (1918) 88 LJ Ch 119).** The subject is also covered In addition, the Local Government Act (LGA) 1972, Schedule 12, paras 10(2)(b) and 26(2)(b) insist that a summons must be left at or sent by post to the usual residence of every member of the council. **The statute additionally insists that the summons (typically by means of an agenda) must specify the business which it is proposed to transact in such a way that the member who receives it can identify the matters which he will be expected to discuss. The full judgement included:**

"It may be that a very important question is going to be

considered at the meeting; it may be on the other hand that the only business is purely formal, paying some tradesman or something of that description. In the one case the members would attend in force and in the other case it was a mere matter of form, the members would not attend beyond the necessary quorum. Accordingly, the notice convening the meeting should contain sufficient description of the important business which the meeting is to transact, and the meeting cannot in ordinary circumstances go outside the business mentioned in that notice"

(The summons is the injunction on councillors to attend the meeting, followed by the agenda for the meeting. It's called a summons rather than an invitation or similar because councillors have a duty to try to attend council meetings).

Another decision was R v The corporation of Dublin (1911) where a special meeting of the corporation was summoned on a requisition of seven ratepayers to consider the question of unemployment in the city and ways and means of alleviating it. At the meeting a resolution was passed authorising the city treasurer to arrange payment of £10,000 on useful works for the alleviation of unemployment. It was held that the notice of the meeting was insufficient to enable the meeting to pass such a resolution. This case gives an indication of how the agenda needs to give a clear and reasonably precise indication of what is to be considered.

SOME USEFUL TIPS

As a Chairman (or Vice Chairman who may have to step in to the chair) You should always check your draft Agendas and Reports before they are distributed to ensure members will have all the available information to make decisions (with due notice). You will want to arrive at Council meetings well before the meetings start. You should go into an office and run through very quickly, the Agenda and Reports with the relevant Officer for the meeting, with the Leader and deputy leader present also, just to make sure you are up to date since they were published, it may be that the Officer is aware of developments that you need to know before the meeting starts, as well as a chance to discuss possible areas of contention, and where it is vital that decisions are made. It helps if the Chairman knows the mind of his Officers and what they need from the meeting.

You should develop a trust with your Officers, you may not always agree, and you are certainly allowed robust political debate, but you should always treat them with dignity and respect. You are also there to protect the Officers in meetings from any undue or unfair criticism, bullying, harassment or derogatory remarks.

Always have with you a copy of the Council's Standing Orders; you may need to consult them, and your officer (usually the Town Clerk should be alert enough to give you guidance as the meeting progresses.)

If someone raises a Point of Order, remember it can only be on procedure, there is no such thing as a point of information, and if in doubt you can always ask the member to point out which Standing Order he is referring to, - to put them on the spot.

Try to encourage participation by inviting members to give comment, this encourages some to come out of their shell and develop better as a councillor and makes others feel valued. Creating a friendly and inviting atmosphere (and thus a likely successful and productive one). May be even ask one or two councillors what do they think!
It is a good idea to generally address councillors formally when meetings are in session. Officers should be addressed by their title.

How to open a meeting: The Chairman sitting in his place, Officers and everyone else in their seats..

Chairman: "Good evening everyone, it has turned 7.15, I declare the meeting open. Can I remind anyone with a mobile phone to switch it to silent..... The first item on the Agenda is apologies for absence,....as per sheet"

Chairman: " Next we have declarations of Interest, has everyone made the necessary declarations for recording in the minutes.

At this point there will be some lazy or late members still scrabbling to complete them, or they may comment ...Remember, as I have amply demonstrated, dual- hatted Councillors sometimes declare a personal interest but unless they "specifically" have a prejudicial (what used to be called pecuniary) interest they can stay and vote. Only the ignorant don't.
A Councillor who is say on the Planning Committee at County Council, can stay and vote and speak at Town Council, all they have to do to protect themselves from any possible conflict whatsoever, is to state " Mr Chairman I wish it to be recorded in the Minutes that on issue blah blah...I will only finally make my mind up at the relevant planning committee meeting at County"   They are thus "totally protected"   from any possible complaints, frivolous, vexatious or otherwise.

 Prejudicial and only prejudicial interests preclude voting or speaking.)

Chairman: "Public Questions as per the Agenda, Mr Town Clerk have we been notified of any questions".

You do not read the full item out like some idiot card, it is printed on the Agenda and every councillor and the public has it in front of them.

Any member of the public with any decency would or should notify the Town Clerk before a meeting commences.

Closing:

Chairman: "that concludes the items on the Agenda, so unless the Officers or members have anything else to say, I thank you for your attendance and close the meeting"

Apart from a very few matters such as the ability to call council meetings, the chairman does not have any more powers than any other councillor. And no councillor has any authority to act on their own unless specifically authorised by the council. A council can only make decisions when it meets as a council, following the usual rules about notice, etc.

VICE CHAIRMEN:

Be ready to take the chair at a meeting whether or not you get the opportunity, know your Agenda and Reports, know the Rules and Procedures and attend the pre-meetings with your Chairman and Officer, the Chairman may have to vacate the chair and you need to be ready to provide a smooth transition. You can also help the chairman by writing down the names of people in front of him so he knows who to call to speak automatically, and can thus concentrate more on the meeting.

TOWN CLERK

The position of Clerk was consolidated by the Local Government Acts of 1888 and 1894 which granted , respectively, County Councils and then Urban and Rural Districts and the newly created civil parish councils the specific power to appoint a "Clerk of the Council". **The importance of the Clerk's position was underlined by Lord Justice Caldecote ruling in Hurle-Hobbs ex parte Riley and another (1944) observed: "The office of town clerk is an important part of the machinery of local government. He may be said to stand between the local Council and the ratepayers. He is there to assist by his advice and action the conduct of public affairs in the** borough and, if there is a disposition on the part of the council, still more on the part of any member of the council, to ride roughshod over his opinions, the question must at once arise as to whether it is not his duty forthwith to resign his office or, at any rate, to do what he thinks right and await the consequences."

(re Hurle-Hobbs ex parte Riley, 20 November 1944, where the Town Clerk, when threatened with dismissal, placed his personal interests above his duty. As in ex parte Riley, duress provides no defence to an allegation of breach of duty; obedience to (unlawful) orders likewise provides no defence; see Attorney General v De Winton (1906) Ch 106 and R v Saunders (1855) 24 LJMC 45 at page 48.) In the case of Attorney-General v De Winton (1906) the court held that a Treasurer (which is what a Chief Financial Officer is) is not merely a servant of the Council, but holds a fiduciary relationship to the tax payer.

Under the section 112 of the Local Government Act (LGA) 1972, a parish or town (local) council shall appoint such officers as necessary for the proper discharge of their functions. In short, it shall appoint a "proper officer". The proper officer is very often referred to as "the clerk (to the council)" but can be known by other terms such as chief executive.

The Town Clerk is not a secretary, or the personal assistant of the chairman or any individual council members. The clerk is employed by, and therefore answerable to, the council as a whole and is instructed to carry out actions by full council or by committees with delegated powers. Town Clerks on a Parish Council, just like Chief Officers of other Local Authorities, have what is called a "Fiduciary Duty" in common law.

It means that their lawful duty is to the Council as a corporate body and the interests of the Council Tax payer, over and above that of the elected Council itself.

This fiduciary duty totally protects him from bullying or harassment where he refuses to act upon or do anything they regard as unlawful. Indeed it is their duty to refuse anything unlawful at all times, even if the whole Council voted for it. He can veto it. And the law fully protects him not the elected councillors. If you want advice on how to proceed on anything you cannot do better than to ask the Town Clerk.

OFFICERS OF THE COUNCIL:

Officers of the Council are responsible day to day to the Town Clerk, no one else. It is the Town Clerk who is responsible for their actions or inactions and no Councillor should ever try to bypass that authority.

Other officers, Finance, Recreation, Environment and so forth assist the Town Clerk to enable the Council to carry out its statutory as well as desired functions as expressed by Council and Committees. They are experts and professionals. That does not mean to say they are always right, after all you will always get any expert in a particular subject to counter or contradict another in the same field. But by and large their advice must be always be heard, and unless good reasons to the contrary, followed. The Council is elected to represent the entire community and add an extra element of common sense.

A good balance is where the Officers advice and guidance is generally followed, and only tempered occasionally by the Elected Councillors who give direction, and priorities as well as overriding in the public interest.

Whilst Officers are usually capable of speaking for themselves it is the absolute duty of any chairman, at meetings, to prevent any abuse, bullying or harassment of officers and staff at all times. In Meetings and outside of them. Robust political argument, and differences of opinion is perfectly correct, but personal attacks and derogatory remarks must never be tolerated.

It is up to Chairmen and Vice Chairmen to show they have a good grasp of the facts, and can generally be trusted to be able to carry the majority of the Committee or Council with them, that way officers will have confidence to act between meetings knowing that common sense will prevail, and that their chairmen and vice chairmen can command the majority of support at a meeting to endorse their actions. Naturally they should always consult with the Leaders of their political group to ensure this process runs smoothly.

Finally, despite becoming a councillor some are rather shy and introvert, it is worth sitting at a table at home and practising a meeting including some of the points above, practice opening and closing, etc, talking to yourself may seem funny but practice a few times in the privacy of your home and it will all start to become a natural behaviour, and easier to do.

GREAT AYCLIFFE TOWN COUNCIL:

SOME USEFUL STANDING ORDERS YOU SHOULD KNOW
(but as these are based on NALC Model Standing Orders they apply to most Councils)

S.O. 1. MEETINGS

(b)(i) When calculating the 3 clear days for notice of a meeting to councillors and the public, the day on which notice was issued, the day of the meeting, a Sunday, a day of the Christmas break, a day of the Easter break or of a bank holiday or a day appointed for public thanksgiving or mourning shall not count.

(b)(ii) The minimum 3 clear days' public notice for a meeting does not include the day on which the notice was issued or the day of the meeting unless the meeting is convened at shorter notice.

(c) Meetings shall be open to the public unless their presence is prejudicial to the public interest by reason of the confidential nature of the business to be transacted or for other special reasons. The public's exclusion from part or all of a meeting shall be by a resolution which shall give reasons for the public's exclusion.

(d)(i) Subject to standing order 1(c) above, members of the public are permitted to make representations, ask questions and give evidence in respect of any item of business included in the agenda of the Council its Committees and specified
Sub-Committees. Questions will not be received by the Council which are in furtherance of a person's individual circumstances or which are about a matter where there is a
right of appeal to the courts, a tribunal or government minister. A question will not be received by the Council, its Committees and specified Sub-Committees where the issue it concerns has been the

subject of a decision of the Council in the last six months.

(d)(ii) With the exception of the Annual or Extra-ordinary Council Meetings members of the public can submit a written question for the Council agenda as long as it is submitted 7 clear days before the Council meeting date. Questions should relate either to the powers and duties of the Council, or affect the Parish in some way. These will be entered on to a register which will be open to the public for inspection.

(e) The period of time which is designated for public participation in accordance with standing order 1(d)(i) and 1(d)(ii) above) shall not exceed 20 minutes.

(f) Subject to standing order 1(e) above, each member of the public is entitled to speak once only in respect of business itemised on the agenda and shall not speak for more than 3 minutes.

(i) A person shall raise his hand when requesting to speak and stand when speaking (except when a person has a disability or it likely to suffer discomfort). The Chairman may at any time permit an individual to be seated when speaking.

(j) Any person speaking at a meeting shall address his comments to the Chairman.

(k) Only one person is permitted to speak at a time. If more than one person wishes to speak, the Chairman shall direct the order of speaking.

(o) The Chairman, if present shall preside at a meeting. If the Chairman is absent from a meeting, the Vice-Chairman, if present, shall preside. If both the Chairman and the Vice-Chairman are absent from a meeting, a Councillor as chosen by the Councillors present at the meeting shall preside at the meeting.

(p) Subject to a meeting being quorate, all questions at a meeting shall be decided by a majority of the Councillors or Councillors with voting rights present and voting.

(q) The Chairman may give an original vote on any matter put to the vote, and in the case of an equality of votes may exercise his casting vote whether or not he gave an original vote.

(r) Voting on any question shall be by a show of hands. At the request of a Councillor, the voting on any question shall be recorded so as to show whether each councillor present and voting gave his vote for or against that question. Such a request shall be made before moving on to the next item
of business on the agenda.

(u) No business may be transacted at a council meeting unless at least one third of the whole number of members of the Council are present. The quorum for Committees, Sub-Committees and Working Groups shall be three members.

4. MOTIONS REQUIRING WRITTEN NOTICE

(a) In accordance with standing order 3(b)(iii) above, no motion may be moved at a meeting unless it is included in the agenda and the mover has given written notice of its wording to the Council's Proper Officer at least 7 clear days before
the next meeting, so that if the meeting is on a Wednesday the Notice of Motion must be received on the Wednesday before.

(b) The Proper Officer may, before including a motion in the agenda received in accordance with standing order 4(a) above, correct obvious grammatical or typographical errors in the wording of the motion.

(c) If the Proper Officer considers the wording of a motion received

in accordance with standing order 4(a) above is not clear in meaning, the motion shall be rejected until the mover of the motion re-submits it in writing to the Proper Officer
in clear and certain language at least 7 clear days before the meeting, so that if the meeting is on a Wednesday the Notice of Motion must be received on the Wednesday before.

(d) If the wording or nature of a proposed motion is considered unlawful or improper, the Proper Officer shall consult with the Chairman of the forthcoming meeting or,
as the case may be, the Councillors who have convened the meeting, to consider whether the motion shall be included or rejected in the agenda.

(e) Having consulted with Chairman or Councillors pursuant to standing order 4(d) above, the decision of the Proper Officer as to whether or not to include the motion in the agenda shall be final.

(f) Notice of every motion received in accordance with the Council's standing orders shall be numbered in the order received and shall be entered in a book, which shall be open to inspection by all Councillors.

(g) Every motion rejected in accordance with the Council's standing orders shall be duly recorded with a note by the Proper Officer giving reasons for its rejection in a book for that purpose, which shall be open to inspection by all Councillors.

(h) Every motion and resolution shall relate to the Council's statutory functions, powers and lawful obligations or shall relate to an issue which specifically affects the Council's area or its residents.

5. MOTIONS NOT REQUIRING WRITTEN NOTICE

(a) Motions in respect of the following matters may be moved without written notice.

i. To appoint a person to preside at a meeting.

ii. To approve the absences of councillors.

iii. To approve the accuracy of the minutes of the previous meeting.

iv. To correct an inaccuracy in the minutes of the previous meeting.

v. To dispose of business, if any, remaining from the last meeting.

vi. To alter the order of business on the agenda for reasons of urgency or expedience.

vii. To proceed to the next business on the agenda.

viii. To close or adjourn debate.

ix. To refer by formal delegation a matter to a committee or to a subcommittee or an employee.

x. To appoint a committee or sub-committee or any councillors (including substitutes) thereto.

xi. To receive nominations to a committee or sub-committee.

xii. To dissolve a committee or sub-committee.

xiii. To note the minutes of a meeting of a committee or sub-committee.

xiv. To consider a report and/or recommendations made by a committee or sub-committee or an employee.

xv. To consider a report and/or recommendations made by an employee, professional advisor, expert or consultant.

xvi. To authorise legal deeds to be sealed by the Council's Common Seal and witnessed.

xvii. To answer questions from Councillors.

xviii. To amend a motion relevant to the original or substantive motion under consideration which shall not have the effect of nullifying it.

xix. To extend the time limit for speeches.

xx. To exclude the press and public for all or part of a meeting.

xxi. To silence or exclude from the meeting a Councillor or a member of the public for disorderly conduct.

xxii. To give the consent of the Council if such consent is required by standing orders.

xxiii. To suspend any standing order except those which are
      mandatory by law.

xxiv. To adjourn the meeting.

xxv. To appoint representatives to outside bodies and to make
      arrangements

for those representatives to report back the activities of outside bodies.

(b) If a motion falls within the terms of reference of a
committee or sub-committee or within the delegated
powers conferred on an employee, a referral of the same
may be made to such committee or sub-committee or
employee provided that the Chairman may direct for it to
be dealt with at the present meeting for reasons of urgency
or expedience.

S.O. 6.   RULES OF DEBATE

(a) Motions and Amendments
(i) All motions or amendments shall be moved and seconded. The Chairman has the authority to require motions or amendments to be given to him/her in writing and signed by the mover.
(ii) Subject to standing order 3(b)(iii) above, a motion included in an agenda not moved by the councillor who tabled it, may be treated as withdrawn.
(b) Seconders Speech
If a member seconding a motion wishes to speak on it later in the debate she/he must indicate this at the time she/he seconds it.
(c) Order of Speaking
The order of speaking shall be determined by the Chairman.
When a member speaks she/he will address the Chairman.
Whilst a member is speaking, no-one else shall speak unless raising a point of order or giving a personal explanation.
(d) Length and Content of Speeches
With the exception of the mover of a motion, no-one shall speak for more than five minutes on any motion unless the Council allows him/her to do so.
Members shall confine the content of their speeches to the subject under discussion.
(e) Member Speaking Again
With the exception of the Chairman, once a member has spoken on a motion she/he can only speak again in the following circumstances:-
(i) If an amendment has been moved.
(ii) If the motion has been amended since she/he last spoke, she/he can move a further amendment.
(iii) If his/her first speech was on an amendment moved by someone else she/he can speak on the substantive motion regardless of whether or not the amendment was carried.
(iv) To exercise the right of reply under Standing Order No. 15 (g).

(v) On a point of order.

(vi) To give a personal explanation.

(f) Amendments to Motions

(i) When an amendment is moved, it shall be dealt with before any further ones are moved. When an amendment is carried it shall become the substantive motion following which further amendments can be moved and dealt with. If no further amendments are moved the Council will then vote on the substantive motion (i.e. either the original motion or the amended one, as the case may be).

(ii) All amendments must relate to the subject matter of the motion. The mover of an amendment must state at the beginning of his/her speech that she/he proposes to put forward an amendment. Amendments must raise issues which are different from those of amendments which have been lost.

They must either add and/or delete words from the motion or refer the motion to a Committee for consideration/reconsideration. Amendments which amount to direct negatives to motions are not permitted.

(iii) A member moving a motion (but not one on which she/he has given notice) can, with the approval of the Council (given without discussion) and his/her seconder, alter the motion if the alteration is one which could be made as an amendment.

(iv) The mover of a motion for the approval of Committee Minutes may if she/he wishes, include suggested amendments to the Minutes.

(g) Right of Reply

The mover of every substantive motion has a right of reply. This is exercised at the close of the debate on the motion, immediately before it is voted upon. The mover of an amendment does not have a right of reply. Where an amendment is moved the mover of the original motion also has a right of reply at the end of the debate on the amendment. This right of reply is confined to answering arguments or objections which have arisen during the debate.

(h) Motions which may be moved during Debate Whilst a motion is being debated the only other motions which can be moved are:-

(i) to amend it;

(ii) to adjourn the meeting;

(iii) to adjourn the debate;

(iv) to proceed to the next business;

(v) that the question be now voted upon;

(vi) under Standing Order No. 5 (a) (xxi) that a member be not allowed to speak any further;

(vii) under Standing Order No. 5 (a) (xxi) that a member should leave the meeting;

(viii) motions to exclude the public under Section 1 (2) of the Public Bodies

(Admission to Meetings) Act 1960.

(i) Closure Motions

(i) If, during a debate, it is moved and seconded that the Council should proceed to the next business, the Mayor will consider this. If she/he agrees she/he will give the mover of the motion the right to reply and will then take a vote on the proposal to proceed to the next business.

(ii) If, during a debate, it is moved and seconded that the question be now voted upon, the Chairman will consider this. If she/he agrees a vote will be taken on the proposal. If it is passed the mover of the original motion will be given a right of reply and his/her motion will then be voted upon.

(iii) If, during a debate, it is moved and seconded that the debate should be adjourned, the Chairman will consider this. If she/he agrees, a vote will be taken on the proposal, but the mover of the original motion will not be given the right to reply.

(j) Points of Order

Members can, at any time, raise points of order.

Points of order relate only to alleged breaches of Standing Orders or statutory provisions and members raising them must specify the Standing Order or statutory provision and why they consider they have been broken.

(k) Personal Explanations

Members can, with the Chairman's permission, give personal explanations on matters referred to by other members.

A personal explanation should be confined to a relevant part of a member's previous speech which may have been misunderstood.

(l) Chairman's Ruling The Chairman's ruling on points of order or personal explanations is final.

(m) Members Speaking: Members will whilst speaking, address other members and officials by their respective titles.

No-one should speak whilst the Chairman is speaking.

Rules are for the guidance of wise men, and shackles for fools.
(Cllr Walter Nunn)

DECLARATIONS OF INTEREST

A member must declare in the meeting if they have any interests, even if already entered on their Register of Interests. This is so that any press and public present can be aware of those interests.

Dual-hatted members and the Code of Conduct

What is a dual-hatted member?
Dual-hatted members are members who serve on two or more relevant authorities; for instance, a member who is both a County and Parish council member. (two or more different Tier Councils)

When should a dual-hatted member declare an interest?

The Code of Conduct does not automatically prevent a Councillor from considering the same matter at more than one tier of local government, including speaking and voting in both tiers. The reference in the Code to members of "any body exercising functions of a public nature" includes other local authorities. The Code says that such dual memberships create a personal interest for any Councillor, which is to be declared only if the member decides to speak. **If an issue is for discussion at both the parish and county level, and Councillors sit on both authorities, they should:**

(a) at the parish level make it clear that they will reconsider the matter at the county level, taking into account all relevant evidence and representations at the County tier; and

(b) at the County level, declare personal (but not prejudicial) interests arising from your membership of the Parish Council, which has already expressed a view on the matter and make it

clear that the Parish Council's view does not bind them and that they are considering the matter afresh.

If a dual-hatted member is taking part in a council meeting and an issue is under discussion which affects that member's other authority, then provided that they do not have a prejudicial interest, under paragraph 9(2) of the Code of Conduct the dual-hatted member only needs to declare a personal interest if they intend to speak on the matter involving the other authority. If the member does speak on the matter then they must declare a personal interest, but they are still able to vote.

Members must consider carefully, however, if the nature of the matter under discussion means that their membership of another authority may also give rise to a prejudicial interest.

For dual-hatted members who would not otherwise have a prejudicial interest for any other reason, a prejudicial interest will arise as a result of membership of the other authority if all of the following conditions are met:
•   the matter affects the other authority's financial position or is about a licensing or regulatory matter applied for by the other authority
•   the matter does not fall within one of the exempt categories of decisions under paragraph 10(2)(c) of the Code
•   a reasonable member of the public with knowledge of the relevant facts would believe that the member's ability to judge the public interest would be impaired

Standards for England takes the view that where a regulatory application, including a matter of consent or approval, is made by a body on a member's register of interests, or a matter is discussed that would impact upon the financial interests of a body on a member's register of interests, then a prejudicial interest will arise. For example if a parish council planning application was being considered at a district council meeting, a member of the planning committee who is also a parish council member would need to declare a personal and prejudicial interest when that matter is considered, leave the chamber and not vote.

Predetermination and dual-hatted members

A dual-hatted member does not automatically have an interest in an item just by virtue of having considered the issue at the meeting of a different authority. If the issue does not meet the normal criteria for needing to declare a personal interest, then an interest does not need to be declared. However, the issue of predetermination or bias may need to be considered where members sit on different bodies determining matters.

Predisposition, Predetermination or Bias, and the Code

Both predetermination and bias have proved to be difficult and controversial issues for many councillors and monitoring officers. Although they are judge-made, common law issues, and not part of the Code of Conduct, Standards for England is publishing this up-dated guide to help clarify the issues.

They originally published a paper on this issue in August 2007. It was based on advice from leading treasury counsel Philip Sales QC.

This new version of the paper aims to clarify the issues involved. It includes examples of where councillors are predisposed, and so can take part in a debate and vote, and where they are predetermined and their participation in a decision would risk it being ruled as invalid.

This area of law is constantly developing which is why the paper has been revised. However, members should refer to their monitoring officers for the most up-to-date position.

What is predisposition?

It is not a problem for councillors to be predisposed to a particular view. That predisposition can be strong and can be publicly voiced.

They may even have been elected specifically because of their views on this particular issue. It might be in favour of or against a particular point of view, for example an application for planning permission.

However, the councillor must be open to the possibility that, however unlikely, they will hear arguments during the debate about the issue that will change their mind about how they intend to vote. As long as they are willing to keep an open mind about the issue they are entitled to take part in any vote on it.

What is predetermination or bias?

Predetermination

is where a councillor's mind is closed to the merits of any arguments which differ from their own about a particular issue on which they are making a decision, such as an application for planning permission. The councillor makes a decision on the issue without taking them all into account.

If councillors are involved in making a decision they should avoid giving the appearance that they have conclusively decided how they will vote at the meeting, such that nothing will change their mind. This impression can be created in a number of different ways such as quotes given in the press, and what they have said at meetings or written in correspondence.

Rarely will membership of an organisation on its own, such as a national charity, amount to apparent bias. This is unless the organisation has a particular vested interest in the outcome of a specific decision that a councillor is involved in making, or the decision is quasi-judicial in nature.

Making the decision

There is an important difference between those councillors who are involved in making a decision and those councillors who are seeking to influence it. This is because councillors who are not involved with making a decision are generally free to speak about how they want that decision to go.

When considering whether there is an appearance of predetermination or bias, councillors who are responsible for making the decision should apply the following test: would a fair-minded and informed observer, having considered the facts, decide there is a real possibility that the councillor had predetermined the issue or was biased?

However, when applying this test, they should remember that it is legitimate for a councillor to be predisposed towards a particular outcome as long as they are prepared to consider all the arguments and points made about the specific issue under consideration.

Also the importance of appearances is generally more limited when the context of the decision-making is not judicial or similar to judicial. Planning decisions are not similar to judicial decisions, they are administrative. Therefore councillors can appear strongly predisposed for or against a particular planning decision.

How can predetermination or bias arise?

The following are some of the potential situations in which predetermination or bias could arise.

Connection with someone affected by a decision

This sort of bias particularly concerns administrative decision-making, where the authority must take a decision which involves balancing the interests of people with opposing views. It is based on the belief that the decision-making body cannot make an unbiased decision, or a decision which objectively looks impartial, if a councillor serving on it is closely connected with one of the parties involved.

Example:

a) A district councillor also belongs to a parish council that has complained about the conduct of an officer of the district council. As a result of the complaint the officer has been disciplined. The officer has appealed to a councillor panel and the councillor seeks to sit on the panel hearing the appeal. The councillor should not participate.

Contrast this with:

b) The complaint about the officer described above is made by the local office of a national charity of which the councillor is an ordinary member and has no involvement with the local office. The councillor should be able to participate in this situation because the matter is not concerned with the promotion of the interests of the charity.

Improper involvement of someone with an interest in the outcome

This sort of bias involves someone who has, or appears to have, inappropriate influence in the decision being made by someone else. It is inappropriate because they have a vested interest in the decision.

Example:

A local authority receives an application to modify the Definitive Map of public rights of way.

A panel of councillors is given delegated authority to make the statutory modification Order. They have a private meeting with local representatives of a footpath organisation before deciding whether the Order should be made. However, they do not give the same opportunity to people with opposing interests.

Prior involvement

This sort of bias arises because someone is being asked to make a decision about an issue which they have previously been involved with. This may be a problem if the second decision is a formal appeal from the first decision, so that someone is hearing an appeal from their own decision. However, if it is just a case of the person in question being required to reconsider a matter in the light of new evidence or representations, it is unlikely to be unlawful for them to participate.

Example:

A councillor of a local highway authority, who is also a member of a parish council that has been consulted about a road closure, could take part in the discussion at both councils. The important thing is that the councillor must be prepared to reconsider the matter at county level in the light of the information and evidence presented there.

Commenting before a decision is made

Once a lobby group or advisory body has commented on a matter or application, it is likely that a councillor involved with that body will still be able to take part in making a decision about it. But this is as long as they do not give the appearance of being bound only by the views of that body. If the councillor makes comments which make it clear that they have already made up their mind, they may not take part in the decision.

If the councillor is merely seeking to lobby a public meeting at which the decision is taking place, but will not themselves be involved in making the decision, then they are not prevented by the principles of predetermination or bias from doing so. Unlike private lobbying, there is no particular reason why the fact that councillors can address a public meeting in the same way as the public should lead to successful legal challenges.

Example 1:

A council appoints a barrister to hold a public inquiry into an application to register a village green. The barrister produces a report where he recommends that the application is rejected. A councillor attends a meeting in one of the affected wards and says publicly: "speaking for myself I am inclined to go along with the barrister's recommendation". He later participates in the council's decision to accept the barrister's recommendation. At the meeting the supporters of the application are given an opportunity to argue that the recommendation should not be accepted.

This is unlikely to give rise to a successful claim of predetermination or bias. The statement made by the councillor only suggests a predisposition to follow the recommendation of the barrister's report, and not that he has closed his mind to all possibilities. The subsequent conduct of the meeting, where supporters of the application could try and persuade councillors to disagree with the recommendation, would confirm this.

Example 2:

A developer has entered into negotiations to acquire some surplus local authority land for an incinerator. Planning permission for the incinerator has already been granted. Following local elections there is a change in the composition and political control of the council. After pressure from new councillors who have campaigned against the incinerator and a full debate, the council's executive decides to end the negotiations. This is on the grounds that the land is needed for housing and employment uses.

The council's decision is unlikely to be found to be biased, so long as the eventual decision was taken on proper grounds and after a full consideration of all the relevant issues.

Predetermination or Bias, and the Code

There is a difference between breaching the Code and being predetermined or biased. It is perfectly possible to act within the Code and still cause a decision you were involved in to be bad for predetermination or bias.

Example:

Under the Code, a councillor may take part in considering whether or not to grant a planning application which is recommended for refusal by planning officers and made by a colleague with whom they do not share a "close association". Nevertheless, because the councillor is the Chair of the planning committee, uses his casting vote to decide in favour of his colleague, and regularly shares a car with that colleague when coming to council meetings, this gives rise to an appearance of bias.

Relationship to the Code of Conduct

The First-tier Tribunal (Local Government Standards in England) in case reference 0352 has also looked at the relationship between the Code and predetermination and gave an indication that where such issues arise there is a potential paragraph 5 Code breach. The outcome is likely to depend on the individual circumstances of a case and any other Code issues and breaches. **This is because a councillor who renders the decision of a council unlawful due to predetermination could reasonably be regarded as bringing that authority or his office into disrepute.**

An important issue for members is that by and large predetermination will not amount to a personal or prejudicial interest. Therefore there is no specific requirement to declare an interest and leave the room under paragraphs 8 to 10 of the Code. **Members may however find themselves the subject of a complaint under paragraph 5 on disrepute. This paragraph of the Code has no provision for declaring interests or leaving meetings.**

Planning decisions are not similar to judicial decisions, they are administrative. Therefore councillors can appear strongly predisposed for or against a particular planning decision.

Commenting before a decision is made

Once a lobby group or advisory body has commented on a matter or application, it is likely that a councillor involved with that body will still be able to take part in making a decision about it. But this is as long as they do not give the appearance of being bound only by the views of that body. If the councillor makes comments which make it clear that they have already made up their mind, they may not take part in the decision.

Conclusion

When making administrative decisions like whether or not to grant planning permission, councillors are entitled to have and express their own views. However, this is as long as they are prepared to reconsider their position in the light of all the evidence and arguments. They must not give the impression that their mind is closed.

MATERIAL PLANNING CONSIDERATIONS:

When a decision is made on a planning application, only certain issues are taken into account; these are often referred to as 'material planning considerations'.

MATERIAL PLANNING CONSIDERATIONS: Issues that may be relevant to the decision (There may exist further material planning considerations not included here)

• Local, strategic, national planning policies and policies in the Development Plan

• Emerging new plans which have already been through at least one stage of public consultation

• Pre-application planning consultation carried out by, or on behalf of, the applicant

• Government and Planning Inspectorate requirements - circulars, orders, statutory instruments, guidance and advice

• Previous appeal decisions and planning Inquiry reports • Principles of Case Law held through the Courts

• Loss of sunlight (based on Building Research Establishment guidance) • Overshadowing/loss of outlook to the detriment of residential amenity (though not loss of view as such)

• Overlooking and loss of privacy

• Highway issues: traffic generation, vehicular access, highway safety

• Noise or disturbance resulting from use, including proposed hours of operation

- Smells and fumes
- Capacity of physical infrastructure, e.g. in the public drainage or water systems
- Deficiencies in social facilities, e.g. spaces in schools
- Storage & handling of hazardous materials and development of contaminated land
- Loss or effect on trees
- Adverse impact on nature conservation interests & biodiversity opportunities
- Effect on listed buildings and conservation areas • Incompatible or unacceptable uses
- Local financial considerations offered as a contribution or grant
- Layout and density of building design, visual appearance and finishing materials
- Inadequate or inappropriate landscaping or means of enclosure

The weight attached to material considerations in reaching a decision is a matter of judgement for the decision-taker however the decision-taker is required to demonstrate that in reaching that decision that they have considered all relevant matters. . Generally greater weight is attached to issues raised which are supported by evidence rather than solely by assertion. . If an identified problem can be dealt with by means of a suitable condition then the Local Planning Authority is required to consider this rather than by issuing a refusal.

NON-MATERIAL PLANNING CONSIDERATIONS:

Issues that are not relevant to the decision: (There exist further non-material planning considerations not included in this list)

- Matters controlled under building regulations or other non-planning legislation e.g. structural stability, drainage details, fire precautions, matters covered by licences etc.
- Private issues between neighbours e.g. land/boundary disputes, damage to property, private rights of access, covenants, ancient and other rights to light etc.
- Problems arising from the construction period of any works, e.g. noise, dust, construction vehicles, hours of working (covered by

Control of Pollution Acts).
- Opposition to the principle of development when this has been settled by an outline planning permission or appeal
- Applicant's personal circumstances (unless exceptionally and clearly relevant, e.g. provision of facilities for someone with a physical disability)
- Previously made objections/representations regarding another site or application
- Factual misrepresentation of the proposal
- Opposition to business competition
- Loss of property value
- Loss of view

Political groups on a Council can make group decisions including on planning (LAW)

Neutral Citation Number: (2006) EWHC 2189 (Admin)
Case No: CO/2586/2005
IN THE HIGH COURT OF JUSTICE
QUEEN'S BENCH DIVISION
ADMINISTRATIVE COURT
Royal Courts of Justice
Strand, London, WC2A 2LL
Date: 25 August 2006
Before:
Mr Justice Collins

- -

Between:

R(Island Farm Development Ltd)   Claimants

v

Bridgend County Borough Council   Defendant

Mr Nigel Jones, Q.C. & Mr David Lawson (instructed by Eversheds)
for the Claimants

Mr Andrew Arden, Q.C. & Mr Christopher Baker (instructed by The
Legal Services Department of the Council) for the Defendant

Hearing dates: 12 - 14 July 2006

Judgment Approved by the Court For handing down

**1.   I have been referred to a number of authorities on the
issue of bias and predetermination. In principle, councillors must
in making decisions consider all relevant matters and approach
their task with no preconceptions. But they are entitled to have
regard to and apply policies in which they believe, particularly if
those policies have been part of their manifestos.** The present
regime believed that the development of the Island Farm site in

accordance with the planning permission was wrong and they had made it clear that that was their approach. In those circumstances, they were entitled to consider whether the development could lawfully be prevented. The fact that a particular policy is included in a manifesto does not mean that it must be implemented. So much was decided by the House of Lords in Bromley LBC v GLC (1983)AC 768. But that case goes no further than deciding that policies which are contrary to law cannot be implemented. That means that they must not contravene any statutory or common law obligation or fail the Wednesbury test. Furthermore, it is important that a judge should not allow his views of the merits of the policy to colour his decision: that would be an unwarranted interference in the democratic process. It follows that in the context of a case such as this I do not believe that bias can exist because of a desire to ensure if possible that the development did not take place. If that approach had been taken, it would have been lawful.

2.   Attempts have in the past been made to impugn decisions of local authorities on the basis that they were driven by a policy imposed by the political party who was in control, and did not consider the merits dispassionately. Most such attempts have failed. An early example is to be found in R v Amber Valley DC ex p Dickson (1985) 1 W.L.R. 2998, a decision of Woolf, J. The case concerned a planning application which the local group of the political party in control had, before it was considered by the relevant committee, resolved to support. Nonetheless, members of the group could not be disqualified from considering the application. Woolf J observed (at p.307):-

"It would be a surprising result if it did (disqualify) since in the case of a development of this sort, I would have thought that it was almost inevitable, now that party politics play so large a part in local government, that the majority group on a council would decide on the party line in support of the proposal. If this was to be regarded as disqualifying the district council from dealing with the planning application, then if that disqualification is to be avoided, the members of the planning committee at any rate will have to adopt standards of conduct which I suspect will be almost impossible to achieve in practice."

He drew attention to the fact that there was an affidavit from the leader of the majority group in which he stated that all material considerations would be taken into account when the planning committee came to deal with the application. This approach is supported by the decision of the Court of Appeal in R v Waltham Forest LBC ex p Baxter (1988) 1 Q.B. 419. That case concerned the decision to set a rate. Prior to the decision, the majority group held a private meeting at which a decision was reached following a vote on the appropriate increase. It was then the duty of the members to vote in accordance with that decision and a number of members who had at the private meeting voted against the increase supported it. It would seem clear that the system did put pressure on members to vote in accordance with party policy notwithstanding that they may not have agreed with it and it may be thought that there was in that respect an element of predetermination. But the Court refused to interfere. Sir John Donaldson MR said this (at p.424H):-

"Mr Wadsworth submitted that in the light of the requirement for rates to be fixed by the Council, the private determination of a group policy in this context did undermine statutory safeguards. I do not agree. So long as councillors are free to remain members despite the withdrawal of the whip and so long as they remember that whatever degree of importance they may attach to group unity and uniformity with group policy, the ultimate decision is for them and them alone as individuals, I cannot see that there is any undermining of statutory safeguards."

The court went on to consider the evidence relating to four individual councillors and accepted that they had acted properly and, in particular, that there was nothing necessarily objectionable in deciding to follow the party line.

112. There is obviously an overlap between this requirement and the commonplace requirement to have rational regard to relevant considerations. But in my judgment, the requirement to avoid predetermination goes further. The further vice of predetermination is that the very process of democratic decision making, weighing and balancing relevant factors and taking account of any other viewpoints, which may justify a different balance, is evaded. Even if all the considerations have passed through the predetermined mind, the weighing and balancing of them will not have been undertaken in the manner required. Additionally, where a view has been predetermined, the reasons given may support that view without actually being the true reasons. The decision-making process will not then have proceeded from reasoning to decision, but in the reverse order. In those circumstances, the reasons given would not be true reasons but a sham.

3.   R(Partingdale Residents Association) v Barnet LBC (2005) EWHC 947 (Admin) is another example of a Councillor having closed his mind to any arguments and having predetermined the relevant decision. Mr Rabinder Singh, Q.C., sitting as a deputy judge, cited observations of McCarthy P in the New Zealand case Lower Hutt City Council v Bank (1974) 1 NZLR 545 @ 550. I need only cite two sentences:-

" ... something less than the scrupulous state of impartiality and its appearance required of a Court of Justice is required of Councils in those circumstances. We think that the state of impartiality which is required is the capacity in a Council to preserve a freedom, notwithstanding earlier investigations and decisions, to approach this duty of inquiring into and disposing of the objections without a closed mind, so that if considerations advanced by objectors bring them to a different frame of mind they can, and will go back on their proposals ..."

4.   Finally, there was Georgiou v Enfield LBC (2004) EWHC 779

(Admin), a decision of Richards J. The decision under attack was to grant listed building consent and planning permission. Members who decided the applications had also been members of the Council's Conservation Advisory Group which had held a meeting before the Planning Committee's meeting in which the forthcoming applications had been considered and voted on. **This was said to give rise to an appearance of bias, based on the principle summarised by Lord Hope in Porter v Magill (2002) 2 A.C. 257 at p.494:-**

"The question is whether the fair-minded and informed observer, having considered the facts, would conclude that there was a real possibility that the Tribunal was biased."

It was accepted by counsel for the local authority that that was the governing principle. He also drew a distinction between bias, predisposition and predetermination, relying on observations of Ouseley J in R(Cummins) v Camden LBC (2001) EWHC 1116 (Admin). The relevant observations are set out in Paragraph 256 of his judgment:-

"There is an important distinction between bias from a personal interest and a predisposition, short of predetermination, arising say from prior consideration of the issues or some aspect of a project. The decision-making structure, the nature of the functions and the democratic political accountability of Councillors permit, indeed must recognise, the legitimate potential for predisposition towards a particular decision. The source of the potential bias has to be a personal interest for it to be potentially objectionable in law."

35. On the other hand, in my view nothing turns on the fact that one of them was the chairman of the planning committee. The problem, as I see it, relates to the possibility that the three members to whom I have referred approached the matter with closed minds, rather than the possibility that they influenced other

members or that the special status attached to the CAG meant that its support for the applications affected other members

I confess to some doubt as to this approach, and in particular to what he says in Paragraph 36. Councillors will inevitably be bound to have views on and may well have expressed them about issues of public interest locally. Such may, as here, have been raised as election issues. It would be quite impossible for decisions to be made by the elected members whom the law requires to make them if their observations could disqualify them because it might appear that they had formed a view in advance. The decision of the Court of Appeal in Baxter's case, of the New Zealand Court of Appeal in the Lower Hutt case and of Woolf J in the Amber Valley case do not support this approach. Nor is it consistent with those authorities that no weight should be attached to their own witness statements. Porter v Magill was a very different situation and involved what amounted to a quasi-judicial decision by the Auditor. In such a case, it is easy to see why the appearance of bias tests should apply to its full extent.

The reality is that Councillors must be trusted to abide by the rules which the law lays down, namely that, whatever their views, they must approach their decision-making with an open mind in the sense that they must have regard to all material considerations and be prepared to change their views if persuaded that they should. It is to be noted that the Court of Appeal sees nothing objectionable in a judge who has refused permission to appeal on the papers sitting on an oral hearing to reconsider his decision. That is because it is recognised that a judge is always prepared to be persuaded to change his mind. So it is with Councillors and, unless there is positive evidence to show that there was indeed a closed mind, I do not think that prior observations or apparent favouring of a particular decision will suffice to persuade a court to quash the decision. This approach is consistent with observations of Lightman J, with which I entirely concur, in R(Loudon) v Bury School Organisation Committee (2002) EWHC 2749 (Admin) in paragraph 23, where he said:-

"The distinction between (disqualifying) pecuniary interests and (non-disqualifying) potential pre-judgment arising from prior publicly stated views in the case of administrative bodies … is well-established: see e.g. R v SSE ex p Kirkstall Valley Campaign (1996) 3 All ER 305. This accords with well-established law in the local authority field where it has long been held that political application and party loyalty and a party whip do not disqualify: see Baxter's case and R v Bradfield MCC ex p Wilson (1989) 3 All E.R. 140."

It may be that, assuming the Porter v Magill test is applicable, the fair-minded and informed observer must be taken to appreciate that predisposition is not predetermination and that Councillors can be assumed to be aware of their obligations. In this case, the evidence before me demonstrates that each member was prepared to and did consider the relevant arguments and each was prepared to change his or her mind if the material persuaded him or her to do so. I am not therefore prepared to accept that there was apparent bias or predetermination which vitiated the decision.

I should perhaps add that some reliance was sought to be placed on the Code of Conduct which applies in England but not in Wales. I accept that continuing membership of a lobby group is inappropriate and that it was correct for Councillor Burns to have resigned from IFAC. But his prior activities did not disqualify him provided that he was prepared to listen to the arguments on the other side and to take all relevant materials into account. The evidence shows that he was so prepared.

It is also material to note that if submissions made by Mr Nigel Jones were correct, the carrying on of local government would be very difficult. Section 13(2) of the Local Government Act 2000 provides that many functions of a local authority are to be the responsibility of an executive of the authority under executive arrangements. Disposal of land is one of the functions which the Cabinet must decide on. If apparent predetermination based on party policy or prior observations is to disqualify, it is difficult to see what could be done since, in the case of this issue, all who are now in control might be regarded as having shown themselves hostile to the development and so the democratic process would be undermined.

It is necessary to bear in mind the nature of the decision being made. In considering whether to sell the land, the committee was concerned only to consider what was in the interest of the Council. And in reaching its decision, immediate financial benefits were not the only consideration. The Committee had to take into account the desirability in the interests of the inhabitants of Bridgend of providing special employment and in maintaining what, after a public inquiry, the UDP had laid down. The existence of planning permission and the effect on the claimants, while no doubt worthy of consideration, could not be given any weight if the conclusion was properly reached that the interests of the Council meant that the land should be retained for future development.

Indeed, since the incoming administration had formed the view that the development was inappropriate, the Committee was not only entitled but bound to look only to what it regarded as the best interests of the Council and inhabitants of Bridgend.
It was in my judgment entitled to decide as it did. Accordingly, this claim is dismissed.
Mr Justice Collins

ELECTION PURDAH

The following is guidance for clarification by me, after a question from a County Councillor I hope it helps as Council Officials are sometimes ambiguous in their advice to Councillors

The relevant guidance is contained in the Code of Recommended Practice on Local Authority Publicity

IN BRIEF: PUBLICITY IN THE PRE-ELECTION PERIOD

The general legal principle set out in the code is that a local authority must not at any time publish any material that in whole or in part appears to be designed to affect support for a political party or a candidate.

When do the restrictions apply?

The restrictions apply six weeks before an election and up to and including the day of the election.

The following points summarise the guidance to councillors and staff.

Business as usual publicity with quotes from appropriate officers not councillors

Reactive publicity can include councillors holding key political or civic positions if commenting in an emergency or a major news event outside the Council's control

Can councillors attend events organised by other organisations?

Councillors can attend events but the same restrictions apply about quoting them in any council publicity.

Councillors can create their own publicity, Councillors can attend events arranged by other organisations, but the same restrictions apply about quoting them in any council publicity Decision-making will continue as usual, and the decisions will be publicised, subject to the restrictions about quotes

Can councillors talk to the press and media during this period?

Of course individual councillors can generate their own publicity during this period subject to their own party's protocols. The restrictions only apply to official council organised publicity including press releases or events.

The rules in the councillor and officer protocols about use of council facilities must be observed.

The Elected Members Code of Conduct now contains a general obligation upon councillors to have regard to the Code of Recommended Practice on Local Authority Publicity. This could mean that any inappropriate use of council facilities during this pre-election period may also be deemed a breach of the Code.

Councillors involved in the election will not be quoted in proactive news releases issued by their Council. Nor should they attend events organised by the council that attract significant numbers of members of the public, or media interest No political posters or leaflets must be displayed on Council premises (including street furniture and the like) or vehicles

This means that any current County or Town Councillor can be called Councillor and can have any publicity in a newspaper, as long as they do not purport to be speaking on behalf of their Council

The only restrictions are that the County Council or Town Council itself, should not be seen in the election purdah period as giving publicity to Councillors seeking re-election.

Guidance for candidates and agents - local government elections in England
http://www.electoralcommission.org.uk/templates/search/docume nt.cfm/17915
Guidance for candidates and agents - local government elections in England: Chapter 3

Newspaper articles and advertisements

3.18 Some newspapers run stories during the election, and feature some or all candidates. While the allocation of broadcasting time is prescribed in legislation, the way that newspapers communicate their views on political issues is not. The inclusion of a candidate in a newspaper article does not count towards election expenses, although paying for an advertisement in a newspaper does.

Advice to Members Serving on Outside Bodies

The point has already been made about the importance of such appointments as part of working in partnership with an increasing range of bodies. The guidance that follows is designed to help you act with confidence and diligence by spelling out your obligations to the organisation concerned. The intention is not to discourage you from seeking appointment but to ensure you understand the position and to reassure you that if you act with due diligence, as you would in relation to your duties as a councillor, then you should have little to fear and much to contribute.

The duties of members appointed to outside bodies cannot be taken lightly and members who are so appointed must take care and carry out their duties to the best of their ability. Such appointments cannot be regarded as mere "figureheads". Responsibilities a member assumes cannot be passed on to others who may have particular functions within the outside body concerned. It is important for members to attend meetings on a regular basis, although some organisations will allow substitutes to attend on an occasional basis.

Members cannot be required to act as delegates and carry out their duties and vote in line with the instructions of the Council; they must act in accordance with their own judgement and the duties and responsibilities set out below. A member's ultimate responsibility is to the terms of the trust, the objectives of an association, or the objectives of the company; the Council can always terminate an appointment if it is unhappy with the performance of a member.

Main Issues:

The primary duty to act in the interests of the outside body

Duties as a trustee (if applicable)

Liabilities in respect of unincorporated organisations

The application of the Council's Code of Conduct

Matters to Check

Members are advised that in the event of being appointed to an outside body they should be clear about the answers to the following questions:

What is the nature of the organisation and its main activities? Is it a company, if so what type of company is it (limited by shares or guarantee)? Is it unincorporated? Does it have charitable status?

In what capacity do I serve on the outside body? Is the effect of my appointment to make me a member of the company, director or a charitable trustee?

Do I have a copy of the body's governing instrument (this may a trust deed, a constitution or memorandum and articles of association)?

Have I been supplied with a copy of any code of conduct to which I am subject as a member of the body?

Am I aware I the identity of other directors, trustees or committee members?

Is there an officer of the body such as secretary or clerk to whom I can refer?

Are written minutes kept of meetings and have I seen these minutes?

Am I aware of the financial position of the organisation to which I have been appointed?

Am I aware of any contracts between the body and the Council?

Do the governing body of the organisation receive regular reports on the financial position?

Have I seen the last annual report and accounts?

Am I aware and have I been advised of the main risks the body faces and what steps are taken to deal with such risks?

Have I been informed of the main insurances held by the body?

Does the Council's indemnity apply to my appointment?

If, having read the guidance, there are issues about which members are unsure or if members encounter any problems and feel that, for instance, they cannot reconcile a conflicting interest, they should seek advice from the Council's officers. Indemnity for Loss

The Council will indemnify members who are appointed to outside bodies where they are exercising a function on behalf of the Council. However, the indemnity provided by the Council acts as a back-stop, where the organisation to which the member has been appointed to by the Council does not itself indemnify or insure the member against any loss or liability. The indemnity provided by the Council is also subject to restrictions which include that the indemnity shall not apply to (i) criminal offences and fraud, (ii) the member must reasonably believe that the act or omission in question was within the powers at the time when he acted, and (iii) does not extend to making claims for defamation.

Any member wishing to take advantage of the indemnity is required (amongst other things) to notify the Council of this fact as soon as is reasonably practicable after the circumstances giving rise to an entitlement claim has come to his/her attention, and to take reasonable steps to mitigate the amount that might otherwise be claimed under the indemnity. Any request for assistance under the indemnity should be made to the Town Clerk to determine whether the indemnity will apply.

2.3 If a member serves on an outside body in a personal capacity, i.e. where he/she is not appointed, or is not doing so at the request of the Council, then the indemnity will not apply.

Further information on the indemnities which can be provided by outside bodies is set out below. As part of familiarising yourself with the aims and objectives of the body, members appointed by the Council to serve on outside bodies in any of the categories listed below should check with the body concerned what indemnities and/or insurance cover, if any, is provided by the body.

Trusts

A trustee should be fully aware of the state of trust property, of the contents of all the deeds and documents relating to the trust, and carry out the terms of the trust in accordance with those documents. Any breach of duty on his/her part may result in him/her being held personally liable. In addition he/she may be personally liable for the acts of his/her co- trustee(s) if his/her own neglect or default contributed to the breach. A trustee must not make use of the trust property or of his/her position as a trustee for his/her own private advantage. It is a general principle that a trustee must not profit from his/her trust and he/she must execute the trust with reasonable diligence and conduct its affairs in the same way as an ordinary prudent person of business.

As a general rule, a trustee is personally responsible for the exercise of his/her judgement and for the performance of his/her duty. He/she cannot escape responsibility by leaving all decisions to be made by another person. Decisions concerning the trust must be taken by all the trustees acting together.

A trustee must usually act impartially and look at the interest of all those who may benefit from the trust. Like a company director, a trustee is expected to act with reasonable prudence and in good faith – the fiduciary duty – in the best interest of the trust and its objects. Trustees must keep an accurate account of trust property and trustees of charities are usually required to submit annual accounts to the Charity Commission. Furthermore, a trustee must usually invest promptly all trust capital and all income which cannot immediately be used for trust purposes.

The Charity Commissioners exercise powers of supervision and control of charitable trustees. If in doubt always consult the Charity Commissioners. A trustee who does so will avoid personal liability for breach of trust if he/she acts in accordance with the advice given. Charitable trustees in breach of certain statutory obligations may be criminally liable e.g. if they recklessly supply misleading information to the Charity Commission, or default in providing the annual report. Also, certain persons are disqualified from acting as charitable trustees. Amongst these are persons with a criminal record for dishonesty, undischarged bankrupts and disqualified company directors.

An indemnity can be given from the trust fund provided the trustee has acted properly and within his/her powers. Trustees may take out insurance to protect themselves against personal liability. Provided that the trustees have authority, they are entitled to be insured against claims that may arrive from their legitimate actions as trustees and will be covered against liability as long as they have acted honestly and reasonable. Again you need to establish what the position is from the Trust itself.

Unincorporated Associations

An unincorporated association consists simply of its members acting together for social reasons, the promotion of politics, sport, art, science or literature or for any other lawful purpose. The property and funds of the association generally belong to the members jointly. The business of the association is either conducted in a general meeting or delegated to committees under the constitution. The members of such committees are usually trustees whose duties and responsibilities are outlined above.

In most cases, an unincorporated association cannot sue or be sued and therefore questions frequently arise about a person's liability for goods supplied to an association, or contracts made on its behalf. The members of an association may be individually liable on contracts entered into by its executive or management committee as authorised by the constitution or because the members themselves specifically agreed to the particular transaction.

There is no limit on liability similar to that which exists for company directors. It is, therefore, essential that members carefully read the constitution of any associations with which they are concerned. Members must keep themselves informed of all financial obligations entered into by the association and ensure that if they disagree with the proposed financial transaction, it is properly recorded in the minutes.

Having sounded this note of caution, many of the unincorporated associations with which members will be concerned do not have their own budgets or become involved in transactions of any kind.

Many are purely advisory or consultative bodies such as the community health councils, and it is most unlikely that any question of personal liability will ever arise.

Members will be entitled to an indemnity from the organisation if they act in accordance with the constitution and are not at fault. It is possible to obtain insurance but if the organisation is to pay the premium it must be permitted by the constitution. In many instances, for the sort of reasons given in the previous paragraph, the organisation may well not have insurance cover.

Council's Code of Conduct
Register of Interests
(a) The Council's Code of Conduct (paragraph 8 (i)(a)) provides that you have a personal interest in any business of your authority where either it relates to or is likely to affect: any body of which you are a member or in a position of general control or management and to which you are appointed or nominated by your authority.
(b) As soon as you have been appointed you must take steps to have your appointment included in the Register of Interests. Any changes must also be notified within 28 days.

Observance of Code
The Council's Code of Conduct (paragraph 2 (5)) requires that where you act as a representative or your authority:-
(a) on another relevant authority, you must, when acting for that other authority, comply with that authority's Code of Conduct; or
(b) on any other body, you must, when acting for that other body, comply with your authority's Code of Conduct except and in so far as it conflicts with any other lawful obligations to which the other body may be subject.

6.3 Conflicts of interests
Members appointed to an outside body will have personal interest in that body and will need to consider their position when

they sit on a council committee or decision making body which is considering a matter to which that interest relates. This may be prejudicial in certain instances, for instance, members participating in a planning or funding decision should declare a personal and prejudicial interest in respect of their membership of the outside body.

The Councillors Code of Conduct :
In the case of ….
"You must treat others with respect".

The Adjudication Panel for England
York House, 31-36 York Place, Leeds, LS1 2ED Tel: 0113 389 6086
www.adjudicationpanel.tribunals.gov.uk
Appeals Tribunal Decision

Case Ref:	APE 0441
Date of Appeal Tribunal Hearing:	10 September 2009
Relevant Standards Committee:	Pendle Borough Council
Date of Standards Committee Decision:	19 May 2009
Name of member concerned:	Councillor David Whipp of Barnoldswick Town Council
Monitoring Officer:	Philip Mousdale
Appeals Tribunal Members:	
Chairman:	Patrick Mulvenna
Member	Darryl Stephenson
Member	David Ritchie

1.   The Appeals Tribunal has considered an appeal from the Appellant about the above decision.

2.   The Appeals Tribunal has considered written submissions from the Appellant and from the Standards Committee.

3.   **The Appellant has appealed against the Standards Committee's finding that the Appellant had failed to follow**

paragraph 3(1) of the Council's Code of Conduct by using the words 'It is you who owe the apology as you are the liars. The CPS got it wrong. You are the guilty ones.' in responding to a question from a member of the public at a meeting of Barnoldswick Town Council ('the Council') held on 10 September 2008.

4.   Paragraph 3 (1) of the Code provides:

"You must treat others with respect".

5.   The Appellant has also appealed against the action which the Standards Committee decided to take in the light of the failure to follow the provisions of the Code of Conduct. That action required him to submit a letter of apology to the Council.

6.   The Appellant has appealed on the grounds that (a) he did not show disrespect by the use of the words he used at the Council meeting; and (b) there were irregularities in the procedures adopted by the Standards Committee. The Standards Committee has responded in detail to the grounds of appeal.

7.   **In relation to the Appellant's ground of appeal that he did not show disrespect, the Appeals Tribunal consider that the approach adopted both by the Investigating Officer and by the Standards Committee was flawed. They have considered simply whether or not the word 'liar' 'went beyond political expression, was rude and offensive and amounted to an expression of anger and personal abuse.' They do not appear to have considered whether or not the Appellant was justified in using the word on the basis that it might be true. In fact, they specifically determined that such possibility did not concern them.**

8.   **There are aspects of the evidence which suggest that the Appellant might have been justified.** The two councillors (Jennifer Purcell and Glenn Robert Whittaker) who have made the complaint against the Appellant and the member of the public whom they

alleged was treated with disrespect (Ms Janet Henderson) were the co-producers and/or authors of the leaflet which gave rise to the Appellant's complaint to the Police. It is evident from the agreed facts that an apology was first sought from the Appellant at the meeting on 10 September 2008 by Councillor Purcell as Councillor Whittaker's election agent. On being prevented from doing so because the business being transacted related to questions from the public, she passed the question to Ms Henderson. Ms Henderson then asked it on Councillor Purcell's behalf effectively, she acted as Councillor Purcell's agent. Having regard to the roles played by all three, it is understandable that the Appellant should address his remark to them collectively.

9.   The leaflet contained inaccurate information in respect of a person who appears to have been identifiable from the information given in the leaflet (Councillor Shelley Franklin although that is not entirely clear from the evidence before the Appeals Tribunal). The Police took the complaint seriously enough to interview persons under caution and to refer the matter to the Crown Prosecution Service, but the Crown Prosecution Service decided not to proceed on the basis (according to DS 1412 Groombridge) that the there was no personal slight in the report of an inflated and exaggerated allowance. It is arguable that the Crown Prosecution Service was wrong: taken as a whole, the leaflet does contain a personal slur by linking the receipt of allowance with an untruthful allegation of failure to attend meetings. It can reasonably be inferred by recipients of the leaflet that the allowances were claimed fraudulently. Ironically, it is the words in the leaflet ascribed to the member of the public, Janet Henderson, who later posed the question to the Appellant which prompted his reply which gave rise to the complaint, which might be considered to be the most injurious. Her's was expressed to be 'the last word' in the leaflet: she referred to 'a Liberal Democrat who takes the money & runs.' It could hardly be more pejorative. The leaflet as a whole could reasonably be construed as containing a 'false statement of fact in relation to (a) candidate's personal character or conduct' which is

the illegal practice to which Section 106 of the Representation of the People Act 1983 relates.

10.   The information contained in the leaflet was clearly intended to affect the return of a candidate at an election and was included in the leaflet at a time when the public generally were becoming more aware of malpractice in the claiming of expenses by those in public office and, with this in mind, must have been calculated to have the most extreme impact on the candidate to whom the information related.

11.   The untruthful information contained in the leaflet, the amount of the allowances claimed and the number of meetings attended, is a matter of public record and it is difficult to see how the wrong information could have been published if those responsible for the publication had exercised the proper duty of care required in such a case, particularly in view of the potential illegal practice to which failure to exercise that duty of care gives rise.

12.   The position was aggravated by the fact that those responsible for the untruthful information acknowledged that the information was false and undertook to take remedial action, but do not appear to have done so. There is no evidence that those who received (and, presumably, accepted the veracity of) the false information were given corrected information or explanations or apologies as to their being misled.

13.   In the light of all these matters the proper course of action for the Appellant was to report the matter to the Police for investigation. It is arguable that he had a duty to do so. There was no justifiable reason to call for an apology for his action. It is little wonder that the Appellant reacted with some apparent loss of control when asked to apologise: the actions of the three persons responsible for the publication of the leaflet had inflamed the atmosphere. It is evident that they had no insight into the enormity

of the implications arising from their action in publishing untruths in electoral material, and appear still to have no insight.

14.   These were all matters which should have been taken into account by the Standards Committee in assessing whether or not the use of the words 'liars' was disrespectful. This would be so whether or not the comments in the leaflet reached the threshold for a prosecution: **it was not open to the Standards Committee to ignore them given their clear relevance to the Appellant's words at the meeting on 10 September 2008. The Committee should have assessed whether or not the untruths could properly be described as lies by exploring whether or not they were deliberate or negligent falsehoods. If they were, the description 'liars' would have been apt and justifiable, albeit unpleasant.**

15.   There is insufficient evidence for the Appeals Tribunal to determine whether or not the Appellant's words were justifiable. There was insufficient evidence before the Standards Committee to make such a determination. **The question which needed to be explored was whether the persons responsible for the publication of the leaflet deliberately and knowingly included false information in the leaflet and manipulated it for electoral gain, or simply made a genuine error which can reasonably be explained. If the answer to the first part of this question is in the affirmative, no reasonable person could consider that there had been disrespect. In the absence of the relevant evidence to answer that question, the decision of the Standards Committee cannot be sustained. The appeal must succeed.**

16.   The Standards Committee have referred to the Case Tribunal's decision in Mason (Needham Market Town Council – APE0427). The Appeals Tribunal is not bound by that decision, but, in any event, the facts can be distinguished. In Mason, the councillor made a pre-meditated attack on the mayor-elect and an officer of the Council. He called them 'proven liars' although there has been no finding by any Court, Tribunal or other competent body

to that effect. **The Appellant in the present case did not initiate an attack but responded to a question. He did not imply that the term 'liar' was other than his own belief.** The Case Tribunal in Mason, acknowledged the relevance of truth in addressing the issue of breaching the Code of Practice. It said (at paragraph 5.3):

'While the truth of comments will often have a direct bearing on whether comments amount to a failure to show respect, in this case the Tribunal was satisfied that the comments of the Respondent were, in the particular circumstances, a breach of the Code whether or not they were true.'

That case turned on its own particular facts, as, indeed must the present case.

17.   The Appeals Tribunal considers, however, that the use of the word 'liars' is inappropriate in the proceedings of a public body even where it does not amount to disrespect. The term is a strong one, which may generally be expected to generate more heat than light in debate. Its use might breach the provisions of the Code of Conduct which require a councillor not to do anything which might bring his office or authority into disrepute. This does not appear to have been considered by the Standards Committee and there is an absence of evidence and submissions on which the Appeals Tribunal can make a determination.

18.   In reaching this view, the Appeals Tribunal has had regard to the fact that the person presiding at the meeting on 10 September 2008 does not appear to have called upon the Appellant to temper his language, to withdraw the remark or to apologise. The only record of anything that ensued is described in Mr Mousdale's report thus: 'There followed what the Clerk describes as a loud and angry exchange between a number of town councillors. The Chairman then moved the meeting onto other business.'

19.   **Moreover, there is insufficient evidence to make an**

assessment of the engagement of Article 10 of the 1950 Convention for the Protection of Human Rights and Fundamental Freedoms which provides:

(1)   Everyone has the right to freedom of expression. This right shall include freedom to hold opinions and receive and impart information and ideas without interference by public authority and regardless of frontiers...

(2)   The exercise of these freedoms, since it carries with it duties and responsibilities, may be subject to such formalities, conditions, restrictions or penalties as are prescribed by law and are necessary in a democratic society, in the interest of ... the protection of the reputation or rights of others...'

20.   Collins J said in Ken Livingstone v The Adjudication Panel for England (2006) EWHC 2533 (Admin), in relation to Article 10, 'the burden is on the (the party interfering with the right) to justify the interference with freedom of speech. **However offensive and undeserving of protection (a person's) outburst may have appeared to some, it is important that any individual knows that he can say what he likes, provided it is not unlawful, unless there are clear and satisfactory reasons within the terms of Article 10(2) to render him liable to sanctions.'**

21.   On the evidence available, it is simply not possible to assess the position and, in any event, if justification could be shown, it would be disproportionate to interfere with the right.

22.   Whilst allowing the appeal, the Appeals Tribunal notes that Mr Mousdale, in his report following his investigation, made reference to the word 'liars' being deemed unparliamentary language in the House of Commons. Local authorities are not bound by the rules of debate adopted by the House of Commons, but the Appeals Tribunal is aware that some local authorities adopt similar rules by custom and practice, if not formally. There is no evidence that there is such a custom and practice in Barnoldswick Town Council, but, whether or not there is, the Appellant might

wish to consider apologising to the Council for breaching the normal rules of debate by the use of inappropriate language.

23.   Having found that there was no sustainable evidence upon which the Standards Committee could properly conclude that there was a breach of paragraph 3(1) of the Code of Conduct, there is no need to reach formal conclusions in respect of the alleged irregularities of procedure. The Appeals Tribunal decided, however, to comment on the allegations so as to address all of the points raised in the appeal.

24.   The starting point in any proceedings which have a judicial or quasi-judicial element is fairness which is a fundamental feature of English law. The guiding principle was expressed by Lord Hewart CJ in R -v- Sussex Justices, ex parte McCarthy (1924) 1KB 256, in the following terms,

'...it is not merely of some importance but is of fundamental importance that justice should not only be done, but should manifestly and undoubtedly be seen to be done.'

25.   In addition, regard must be had to Article 6 the 1950 Convention for the Protection of Human Rights and Fundamental Freedoms as given effect in English law by the Human Rights Act 1998 which gives a right to a fair trial.

26.   The Appeals Tribunal does not consider that any useful purpose would be served by reviewing in detail the merits of each allegation but has simply commented on what might be considered to be good practice in respect of the matters raised. The following are the main issues:

26.1.   The presence on the Standards Committee of Councillors Simpson and Starkie who the Appellant claimed were biased. It is evident that the alleged bias was   considered to some degree, but it appears that the Appellant was prevented at the hearing from

74

expressing the reasons for alleging bias. **The Appeals Tribunal considers a Standards Committee has a duty to consider any allegation of bias and should hear those allegations. The duty is a continuing** one and is relevant in relation to the bias shown at a hearing. It is good practice for a Standards Committee to ensure that its proceedings are free from actual bias or perceived bias. In this respect, a Committee should take a proactive role rather than relying on individuals to declare interests.

26.2. The Chairman of the Standards Committee was alleged to have treated the Appellant and his representative unfairly and to have constantly interrupted. It is the Chairman's duty to exercise control and ensure that the proceedings are run smoothly and efficiently. It requires a fine balance and support from competent advisers. It appears that this was present at the hearing.

26.3. The Standards Committee are alleged not to have considered the relevance of the evidence to be given by potential witnesses. The Appeals Tribunal considers that a Standards Committee has a duty to consider such relevance and to give reasons for not calling witnesses. The same considerations apply to an Investigating Officer's refusal to interview potential witnesses.

26.4. The Appellant has suggested that the investigating officer should have been in a position to give evidence. The role of the Investigating Officer is a difficult task and he needs to be in a position in which he can act impartially at all times. It is evident that Mr Mousdale carried out his investigation in the present case with the highest degree of integrity and diligence and, as Monitoring Officer, he was the obvious choice for the role. The Appeals Tribunal would not seek to impugn the investigation in the present case, but offers the following comment to address the issue raised by the Appellant. If a person does have knowledge which would assist by way of evidence or has played any material role in the circumstances given rise to the complaint, he should not be appointed as Investigating Officer. It would be good practice to have in place a reciprocal arrangement with neighbouring authorities to provide Investigating Officers when there is clear difficulty in using the authority's own officers.

26.5. The circulation of papers prior to the hearing is a fundamental requirement, as is ensuring that all persons have access to the same documentation. It is not unreasonable to assume that a party will have copies of documents he has provided. However as a matter of good practice, paginated bundles should be prepared for all parties and members of the Standards Committee.

26.6. It is desirable that any investigations and consequential proceedings should be undertaken with the minimum of delay, particularly if any delay prejudices a party by the timing of a decision. It is not clear from the evidence whether or not there was any inordinate or unreasonable delay in this case.

27. The Appeals Tribunal has allowed the appeal. The decision was unanimous.

28. The decision of the Standards Committee ceases immediately to have effect.

29. A copy of this determination is being given to the Appellant, the Standards Board, the Standards Committee and any person who made the allegation that gave rise to the investigation.

30. This determination will be published in a newspaper circulating in the area of the local authority and will also be published on the Adjudication Panel's website at www.adjudicationpanel.tribunals.gov.uk.

Patrick Mulvenna
Chairman of the Appeals Tribunal
14 September 2009

Jurisprudence about the need for politicians to have thicker skins than others. (LAW)

The Monitoring Officer got it wrong ! Councillors rights to free speech, enhanced protection of Councillors under Article 10 (1 & 2)

Neutral Citation Number: (2012) EWHC 1172 (Admin)
Case No: CO/10054/2011
IN THE HIGH COURT OF JUSTICE
QUEEN'S BENCH DIVISION
ADMINISTRATIVE COURT IN WALES
Cardiff Civil Justice Centre
2 Park Street, Cardiff, CF10 1ET
03/05/2012
B e f o r e : THE HONOURABLE MR JUSTICE BEATSON
___Between:

The Queen on the application of Lewis Malcolm Calver Claimant
- and -
The Adjudication Panel for Wales   Defendant
- and -
Public Services Ombudsman for Wales   Interested Party

Robert McCracken QC and Matthew Paul (instructed by William

Graham Law) for the Claimant
The Defendant did not appear and was not represented
Gwydion Hughes (instructed by Public Service Ombudsman for Wales) for the Interested Party

Hearing date: 3 April 2012
Crown Copyright ©
Mr Justice Beatson :

1.   These proceedings concern the restrictions on the conduct of members of local authorities and thus to their right to freedom of expression introduced as a result of the Third Report of the Committee on Standards in Public Life (Cm 3762, July 1997) to promote and uphold proper standards in local democracy. At the material times the claimant, Lewis Malcolm Calver, was a member of Manorbier Community Council. Manorbier is a tourist resort in South Pembrokeshire with a permanent population of about 700. The claimant was elected to its Community Council in 2004 in a contested election. In May 2008 all the candidates for the vacancies on the Community Council including the claimant were returned unopposed. In that year he was also re-elected to the Pembrokeshire County Council for a ward which includes Manorbier.

2.   As a member of the Community Council, the claimant was required to undertake to abide by its Code of Conduct, adopted pursuant to the Community Council's statutory obligations under the Local Government Act 2000 ("the 2000 Act"). Paragraphs 4(b) and 6(1)(a) of the Code of Conduct respectively require members to "show respect and consideration for others", and not to "conduct (themselves) in a manner which could reasonably be regarded as bringing (their) office or authority into disrepute".

3.   In this application, the claimant challenges the decision of the Adjudication Panel for Wales ("the Panel"), dated 25 May 2011 to dismiss his appeal against the decision of Pembrokeshire County Council's Standards Committee ("the Standards Committee") on 5

November 2010. The Standards Committee had decided that a number of comments or blogs posted by him on www.manorbier.com, a website he owned and wholly controlled, between June 2008 and May 2009, breached paragraphs 4(b) and 6(1)(a) of the Code of Conduct. It censured him and required him to attend a training session with the Council's Monitoring Officer.

4.   These proceedings were lodged on 19 October 2011. Permission was granted following an oral hearing before HHJ Curran QC on 26 February 2012 at which issues of delay were considered. The defendant filed an Acknowledgement of Service but has not appeared. Mr Gwydion Hughes has, however, made submissions in favour of upholding the decision of the Panel on behalf of the Public Service Ombudsman for Wales (hereafter "PSOW"), who instigated the investigation of the claimant and referred his case to the Standards Committee.

5.   **The overarching question before the court is whether the defendant's decision that the claimant's comments put him in breach of the Code of Conduct erred in law or is otherwise flawed in public law terms. The answer to that question principally depends on whether the Panel's decision failed to give sufficient weight to the claimant's right to free expression under the common law and Article 10 of the European Convention of Human Rights(1) ("the Convention"). This in turn involves considering whether the defendant erred in finding the comments did not constitute political expression attracting an enhanced level of protection under Article 10, and whether or not they attract that enhanced level of protection, whether the decision that thirteen of the comments broke the Code of Conduct and to censure the claimant was a disproportionate interference with his right under Article 10. The subsidiary issues include the effect of the claimant's undertaking to abide by the Code of Conduct, as he was required to do in order to be a Councillor, and whether the Code of Conduct can be interpreted so as to give full effect to his right to free expression under Article 10, and, if not whether the Code**

itself is ultra vires.

The legal framework

6.   The Manorbier Community Council's Code of Conduct was issued as part of the framework created by Part III of the Local Government Act 2000 ("the 2000 Act"), as a result of the third report of the Committee on Standards in Public Life (CM 3702-1) in 1997. The report recommended a new ethical framework for local government in order to promote and uphold proper standards in public life, and the 2000 Act made provision for this. The framework includes (section 53) Standards Committees, whose functions are (section 54) to promote and maintain high standards of conduct by members and co-opted members of relevant authorities. It also includes model Codes of Conduct.

7.   Some of the provisions of the 2000 Act apply to England and Wales, but others make separate provision for Wales: see for example sections 5(4) and (5), 7, 9(2), 49(2) (4) and (5), 50(2), 51(6)(c)(ii), 54(5) and (7), and 69-74. The framework and the model Code of Conduct applicable in Wales thus differ in a number of respects from those applicable in England. The 2000 Act has also been amended by the Public Audit (Wales) Act 2004, Public Services Ombudsman (Wales) Act 2005, and the Local Government and Public Involvement in Health Act 2007 ("the 2007 Act"). References to the 2000 Act are to the Act as amended.

8.   The framework under the 2000 Act applicable in England and its relationship to Article 10 has been considered by this court in Sanders v Kingston (2005) EWHC 1145 (Admin); Livingstone v Adjudication Panel for England (2006) EWHC 2533 (Admin) and R (Mullaney) v Adjudication Panel for England (2009) EWHC 72 (Admin). The first two decisions were statutory appeals against decisions of case tribunals pursuant to section 79(15) of the 2000 Act. The third was an application for judicial review of the decision of the Adjudication Panel for England, the body which hears appeals from decisions of the Standards Committees of English relevant

authorities.

9.   Changes were introduced by the 2007 Act following the Tenth Report of the Committee on Standards in Public Life (CM 6407) in 2005 and the decision of Collins J in Livingstone v Adjudication Panel for England in 2006. In the case of Wales (but not England) one purpose was to make it clear that parts of the framework governing members of a relevant public authority apply at all times but other parts apply only where that person acts, claims to act or gives the impression that he or she is acting in the role of member or representative of the public authority in question: see sections 49(2D), 50(4E) and 51(4C) of the 2000 Act.

10.   Sections 49 and 51 of the 2000 Act require relevant public authorities in Wales to adopt the model Code of Conduct issued by the National Assembly for Wales regarding the conduct which is expected of members of relevant public authorities in Wales, or a Code in very similar terms. The Manorbier Community Council is a relevant authority by virtue of section 49(6)(f) of the 2000 Act. In the case of both England and Wales, as a result of section 183(4) of the 2007 Act, section 52 provides that a member of a relevant authority must, within two months of the date on which the Code is adopted, give the authority a written undertaking that he will observe the authority's Code of Conduct, and if he fails to do so will cease to be a member of the authority at the end of the period. One of the differences between the framework in Wales and that in England is seen in the parallel texts of section 52 of the 2000 Act about the duty of members and co-opted members of relevant authorities to comply with the model Code of Conduct. In the case of England, but not Wales, the duty is expressly limited to the performance by the member or co-opted member of "his functions".

11.   The Conduct of Members (Principles) (Wales) Order 2001 SI 2001 No. 2276 (W.166) specifies the principles which are to govern the conduct of members and co-opted members of relevant

authorities in Wales. There are ten principles; "selflessness", "honesty", "integrity and propriety", "duty to uphold the law", "stewardship", "objectivity in decision-making", "equality and respect", "openness", "accountability" and "leadership". Principle 7, "equality and respect", provides:

"Members must carry out their duties and responsibilities with due regard to the need to promote equality of opportunity for all people, regardless of their gender, race, disability, sexual orientation, age or religion, and show respect and consideration for others."

The "selflessness" principle prohibits members from using their position as members to improperly confer advantage on themselves. The "leadership" principle requires them to "respect the impartiality and integrity of the authority's statutory officers and its other employees".

12.   The equivalent provisions for England are contained in the Relevant Authorities (General Principles) Order 2001 SI 2001 No. 1401. The formulation of the principles differs in a number of material respects. For example, the promotion of equality and respect for the impartiality and integrity of an authority's officers and employees are dealt with under the 'Respect for Others' principle. Also that principle, unlike the Welsh 'Equality and Respect' principle, contains no reference to 'consideration' for others, only to 'respect'.

13.   Provisions for investigations by the PSOW are made in chapter III of Part III of the 2000 Act. By section 69(1)(b), the PSOW may investigate of his or her own motion in cases in which he or she "considers that a member or co-opted member (or former member or co-opted member) of a relevant authority in Wales has failed, or may have failed, to comply with the authority's Code of Conduct and which have come to his attention as a result of an investigation under paragraph (a)". Section 69(1)(a) concerns investigations in cases in which a written allegation is made to the PSOW by any person about the failure of a member or co-opted member of

relevant authority to comply with the authority's Code of Conduct.

14.   Section 69(3) of the 2000 Act provides that the purpose of an investigation is to determine which of the findings mentioned in sub-section (4) is appropriate. Sub-section (4) lists four findings. That relevant in the present context is section 69(4)(c), that the findings are "that the matters which are subject of the investigation should be referred to the Monitoring Officer of the relevant authority concerned".

15.   Section 73(1) of the 2000 Act provides that the National Assembly for Wales may make regulations "in relation to the way in which any matters referred to the monitoring officer of a relevant authority under...section 71(2)...are to be dealt with". By section 73(4)(c), the Regulations may make provision "conferring a right of appeal on a member or co-opted member of a relevant authority in respect of any action taken against him". The Local Government Investigations (Functions of Monitoring Officers and Standards Committees) (Wales) Regulations 2001 SI 2001 No. 2281 (W.171) provide that the appeal lies to an Appeal Tribunal drawn from the Adjudication Panel for Wales.

16.   The current model Code of Conduct issued by the National Assembly for Wales is contained in the Local Authorities (Model Code of Conduct (Wales)) Order 2008, SI 2008 No. 788 (W.82). It came into force on 18 April 2008, replacing the earlier 2001 Model Code of Conduct, S1 2001 No. 2289 (W.177).

17.   The material provisions of the Manorbier Community Council's Code of Conduct are:
"2(1)...You must observe this Code of Conduct ...
(a) whenever you act, claim to act, or give the impression you are acting in the role of member of the authority to which you were elected or appointed;
(b) whenever you act, claim to act, or give the impression you are acting as a representative of your authority; or

(c) at all times and in any capacity, in respect of conduct identified in paragraphs 6(1)(a) and 7."

...

4. You must

...

(b) show respect and consideration for others;

...

6(1). You must
(a) not conduct yourself in a manner which could reasonably be regarded as bringing your office or authority into disrepute."

18.   Paragraph 4(b) of the Code, requiring members to "show respect and consideration for others", thus only applies where a member of the Council acts, claims to act, or gives the impression that he or she is acting in the role of a member of the Community Council, but paragraph 6(1)(a) of the Code applies at all times to a member of the Council, whatever he or she may be doing.

19.   Article 10 of the European Convention of Human Rights ("the Convention") provides:
"(1) Everyone has the right to freedom of expression. This right shall include freedom to hold opinions and to receive and impart information and ideas without interference by public authority and regardless of frontiers....
(2) The exercise of these freedoms, since it carries with it duties and responsibilities, may be subject to such formalities, conditions, restrictions or penalties as are prescribed by law and are necessary in a democratic society, in the interests of...the protection of the reputation or rights of others, ..."

20.   Convention Rights, including Article 10, are given direct effect in domestic law by the Human Rights Act 1998. Section 6 of that Act provides that it is unlawful for a public authority to act in a way which is incompatible with inter alia Article 10 (save in limited circumstances concerning primary legislation). Section 3 provides that legislation and subordinate legislation, so far as it is

possible to do so, must be read and given effect in a way which is compatible with the Convention rights.

21.   In limiting what a member of a relevant authority may say and do, the provisions of the 2000 Act and the Codes of Conduct made under it restrict the rights of members to free expression under Article 10. Neither in this case nor in the cases to which I have referred in (8) was it contended that the legislative scheme making provision for codes of conduct in itself constitutes a breach of Article 10. Accordingly, and subject to one qualification, the principal questions are whether the undoubted restriction on the Article 10 rights of councillors in the Code, as applied by the Panel to the comments the claimant posted on his website, falls within Article 10(2) and is justified in the circumstances of this particular case either on a purely common law interpretation of the relevant provisions of the Manorbier Community Council's Code of Conduct, or as a result of the operation of section 3 of the Human Rights Act 1998. The qualification concerns the difficulty in practice of maintaining the analytical distinction between a purely common law interpretation and that achieved as a result of section 3: see (46).

The factual background

22.   Prior to 2008 there were concerns about the way Manorbier's Community Council operated, particularly in respect of financial management. Those concerns had been expressed to Pembrokeshire County Council's monitoring officer and to other officials. In a letter dated 26 February 2009 to the PSOW, the Monitoring Officer stated that, in the period before the 2008 election, the Council "had been considered a failing Council by many".

23.   In September 2005 the claimant asked the PSOW to conduct a major investigation into the affairs of the Council. The PSOW declined, stating that his role was to investigate specific allegations

that members had breached the Council's Code of Conduct. In 2006 the Council was successfully sued by a marketing company for breach of a contract to conduct a survey. It also dismissed its clerk in circumstances which led to proceedings against it in the Employment Tribunal. In July 2006 the claimant complained to the PSOW about the refusal to provide him with details of the advice given to the Council about the dismissal of its clerk. In a letter dated 15 August, the Ombudsman's office stated the matter fell outside his remit because the claimant was complaining in his capacity as a Community Councillor rather than as a member of the public.

24.   In early 2008, as part of their opposition to a planning application relating to an estate in the Community Council's area, Cllr Gourlay and another Councillor made use of a video showing a child being abducted. This was later referred to by the Chairman of the Pembrokeshire National Park Planning Committee as "being like a video nasty", and representing "child manipulation": see Western Telegraph, 26 March and 4 April 2008. The claimant's posted comments on his website included comments on this matter, one of which was among those found by the defendant to breach the Code of Conduct.

25.   I have referred to the fact that, because insufficient candidates were nominated to serve on the Community Council in 2008 to require an election, those who were nominated were returned unopposed. The claimant (who at that time had been a member of the Community Council for approximately 10 years) and Cllr Gourlay, who became responsible for preparing the minutes of Council meetings, were two of the councillors returned in this way. Four other members of the Community Council subsequently resigned because of what they described as the lack of enthusiasm of electors to serve on the council.

26.   After the 2008 election the relationship between the claimant and other members of the Community Council was bad. In the submissions to the Panel on behalf of the PSOW it was stated

(decision report, paragraph 3.2.7) that the Council was "a disaster zone" and that "relations between Community Councillors appear to have broken down". Relations appear to have been particularly bad between the claimant and the Chair, Cllr Hughes, and Cllr Gourlay. Cllr Hughes had unsuccessfully contested the election to the County Council in which the claimant was elected. In a letter dated 3 March 2009 to the PSOW, Cllr Gourlay claimed she had been subjected to intense ridicule.

27.   The comments posted on the claimant's website contained in the court bundle appear to cover the eleven month period between June 2008 and May 2009. The claimant sought and received advice from Mr Huw Miller, head of Legal and Committee Services at Pembrokeshire County Council, about publishing draft minutes of the Community Council on his website. On 1 September 2008 the Community Council passed a resolution stating that no minutes should be published until they were approved by the Community Council. Councillors on Manorbier Community Council received training from Pembrokeshire County Council's Monitoring Officer on the Code of Conduct at a meeting on 8 December 2008.

28.   There were disputes between the claimant and others as to inter alia: the adequacy of notice of meetings, the quality and adequacy of the minutes of meetings, and declarations of interest. There were also disputes about what the claimant saw as a mistaken view by some other councillors of his role as a County Councillor. The only evidence before the court is by or in support of the claimant. His evidence is that the view of some was that, because the electoral division that he represents on the County Council includes Manorbier, he should represent the Community Council's views on the County Council rather than exercise his judgment as to the interests of the county. A resident, a Mr Tew, stated that there were bad tempered remarks made to the claimant by other councillors, including that he would be silenced, and that proposed amendments to minutes by him were "nit-picking". The claimant stated that Cllr Hughes' behaviour to him was intimidating

and threatening.

29.   In 2009 three Councillors, including Cllrs Hall and Gourlay, were granted dispensations to debate and vote on business concerning the Manorbier Community Association. They had declared that they held no position of responsibility or management on that Association, whereas in fact they sat on its General Management Committee. In May 2009 the Community Council passed a motion of no confidence in the claimant. The motion was proposed by Cllr Hughes and carried by the exercise of his casting vote as chairman. That year the Community Council settled the wrongful dismissal claim brought by its former clerk in 2006 by making a substantial payment.

30.   On 19 October 2009 the claimant complained to the PSOW that Cllr Hughes had breached the Code of Conduct. He alleged that Cllr Hughes had failed to declare a prejudicial interest in relation to two Community Panel workshops held in September 2008 and September 2009, and in nominating himself to attend a meeting of the Pembrokeshire Coast National Park Authority without declaring an interest that arose because of Cllr Hughes's ownership of certain land. The PSOW did not report on this complaint until 24 February 2011. In his report he stated that he considered that Cllr Hughes had breached the Code of Conduct in these matters, and referred them to Pembrokeshire County Council's Standards Committee. In a decision dated 27 September 2011 the Standards Committee resolved that Cllr Hughes should have declared a personal and prejudicial interest, and should have left the meeting for an item concerning the local development plan. It also found that he had breached the Code of Conduct by not withdrawing from the two Panel meetings. It, however, resolved that no action be taken.

31.   I return to the chronology. In the course of his investigation into the claimant's complaint against Cllr Hughes, the PSOW discovered that the claimant was running the www.manorbier.com website. The website included comments, amongst other things,

about the functions and activities of the Council and about individual members of the Council. The PSOW considered that a number of the claimant's posted comments could constitute breaches of the Code of Conduct. Accordingly, he exercised his powers under section 69(1)(b) of the 2000 Act to start an investigation into the claimant's conduct. On 20 April 2010, he issued a report in which he found that there was prima facie evidence that the claimant had committed forty-three breaches of the Code of Conduct. He referred the report to the Standards Committee of Pembrokeshire County Council.

The decision of the Standards Committee

32.   The matter first came before the Standards Committee on 28 September 2010. As a result of late information being presented, the meeting was adjourned to 5 November 2010. After a public hearing the Standards Committee found breaches of the Code by the claimant in respect of thirteen comments. It found that there was no evidence to prove that he had disclosed confidential information in breach of paragraph 5(a) of the Code, and insufficient evidence of bullying or harassment by him in breach of paragraph 4(c). But it found that there was evidence: (a) to prove that he had failed to show respect and consideration to others in breach of paragraph 4(b), and (b) to support a finding that he brought the Manorbier Community Council into disrepute in breach of paragraph 6(1)(a) of the Code.

33.   The key parts of the comments posted on the website on various dates in relation to which the Standards Committee found there was evidence of breaches of the Code of Conduct (with the paragraph(s) of the Code of Conduct which the Committee found were breached in brackets) are:

(1) "Manorbier Community Council does not seem to understand the limits of its role. This lack of understanding is difficult to comprehend following the advice received from Lawrence Harding the Pembrokeshire County Council Monitoring Officer." (Code, paragraph 6(1)(a)).

(2) "Anybody who attended the October meeting would have great difficulty in relating the actual events to the draught (sic) minutes above. Anybody looking at these minutes at some time later, such as next year, would not have any ideas to what was agreed, discussed or expenditures approved. The draught (sic) has just blown the facts away. There are more holes in the Draught (sic) Minutes than in Swiss Cheese." (Code, paragraphs 4(b) and 6(1)(a)).

(3) "Ms Gourlay has tried many times to be elected by ballot and failed. She has succeeded in becoming a Councillor as no ballot was had". (Code, paragraphs 4(b) and 6(1)(a)).

(4) "Disgraceful manipulation of children (by Mr Wales – now ex Councillor) to influence a lawful planning application. Mr Wales...has now left (Manorbier Community Council) leaving the Council in a mess." (Code, paragraph 6(1)(a))

(5) "Councillor Gourlay at this stage states that she was an expert on declarations of interest. It is not known where Councillor Gourlay acquired her expertise (or her present place of employment?." (Code, paragraph 4(b)).

(6) "Manorbier Community Council as a ship will sail on until members of the Community realise how much of their money has been wasted over the last year and how much dealing has been carried out in secret meetings." (Code, paragraph 6(1)(a)).

(7) "... the past two and a half years in the absence of a competent clerk has proved very costly to the ratepayers of Manorbier." (Code, paragraphs 4(b) and 6(1)(a)).

(8) "Manorbier Community Council both in the recent past and in the present seems to live in the land of secrecy with many skeletons in the cupboard which will eventually come out." (Code, paragraph 6(1)(a)).

(9) "The staffing committee has with the indulgence of other past Councillors...cost the charge payers of Manorbier in excess of £55,000." (Code, paragraph 6(1)(a)).

(10) "Manorbier Community Council meeting, Monday 1st September Manorbier Councillors through its Chairman strive to stop this website publishing draft minutes of Council meetings...the reason this website published the draft minutes is to show their

poor quality and it will not be browbeaten by anyone who wishes to inflict censorship...Cllr Hughes informed Cllr Calver that he was not prepared to supply him with signed corrected minutes using the feeble excuse that somebody might forge his signature...perhaps both Cllr Hughes as Chairman and Cllr Williams, the deputy chairman (who is believed to have been an ex-headmaster) should have been concerned about the standard of the draft minutes that were being displayed on this website and described by Mr Crocker as being of poor quality. One can only wonder at the statement by the chairman that the council would have collapsed had Ms Gourlay not volunteered for the role where she acted firstly as the Proper Officer and secondly as the writer of the minutes...resigning as Proper Officer in her letter to the council." (Code, paragraphs 4(b) and 6(1)(a)).

(11) "For a Chairman of a Community Council who has just had the benefit of being trained to suggest that he would not provide signed copies of council meetings to fellow councillors beggars belief, perhaps he beliefs (sic) that he is above the law of the land which states that the minutes of council meetings have to be signed 'as being a true and accurate record of the meeting' and then become placed in the public domain and open to inspection by any member of the public." (Code, paragraph 6(1)(a)).

(12) "The website will of course continue to publish both draft and the agreed signed minutes with or without the co-operation of the Council." (Code, paragraphs 4(b) and 6(1)(a)).

(13) "...In regard to the 'backdoor' method of becoming a Councillor...not one Councillor, so far, has actually been elected to represent the people." (Code, paragraph 6(1)(a)).

In the remainder of this judgment I identify the comments by the bracketed number at the beginning of each of them.

34.   The summary shows that the Committee considered that, in respect of five of the thirteen comments, (2), (3), (7), (10) and (12), there was evidence to prove that the claimant had breached both paragraphs 4(b) and 6(1)(a). It considered that in respect of one comment, (5), there was evidence to prove that the claimant had

breached only paragraph 4(b). As to the six other comments, the Committee considered there was evidence to prove that the claimant breached paragraph 6(1)(a). It is to be recalled (see (17) – (18)) that paragraph 6(1)(a) applies at all times to a member of a Council whether or not he or she is acting as a member of a Council. The Committee stated that it considered that the paragraphs identified "had been breached by virtue of the cumulative effect of the evidence presented, which undermined the confidence of Councillors and the authority of Manorbier Community Council".

35.   The Standards Committee resolved that the claimant be censured and required to attend a training session with Pembrokeshire County Council's Monitoring Officer within 3 months. The Committee also considered it would be beneficial for all other members of Manorbier Community Council to receive a joint training session by the Monitoring Officer. It also stated that it hoped that the Council would operate in a more cohesive way, and that the claimant would consider carefully the language used on his website in the future.

36.   The claimant appealed to the defendant Panel on the following grounds. First, he maintained he was not acting in his official capacity as a Councillor, or in any way misusing his position as Councillor, in making the comments which were the subject of the complaint. Secondly, he argued that the comments singly or taken together were incapable of bringing the Community Council into disrepute, and did not demonstrate a lack of respect or consideration for others. It was argued on his behalf that any reporting on the website of discreditable behaviour by the Council or individual Councillors was "truthful and factually accurate", the comments were "legitimate political comment on the actions" of the Council or individual Councillors, and that the finding that the comments breached the Code was an unnecessary and disproportionate infringement of the claimant's right to free expression under Article 10 of the European Convention on Human Rights. The grounds of appeal thus track very closely the grounds

upon which these proceedings are brought.

The decision of the Panel

37.   The Panel heard and unanimously dismissed the claimant's appeal on 25 May 2011. It is that decision which is challenged in these proceedings. Both the claimant and the PSOW were represented before the Panel by counsel. The Panel had before it a number of decisions, including those in Sanders v Kingston (2005) EWHC 1145 (Admin), Livingstone v. Adjudication Panel for England (2006) EWHC 2533 (Admin), and R (Gaunt) v Office of Communications (2011) EWCA Civ 692. The material parts of the Panel's decision are:

"3. The allegations considered by the Appeal Tribunal were that Cllr Calver had breached Manorbier Community Council's Code of Conduct by publishing derogatory website comments about two fellow Community Councillors, and by bringing his office and/or Manorbier Community Council into disrepute.

...

5. At a hearing on 25 May 2011 at the Lamphey Court Hotel, Lamphey, Pembrokeshire, the Appeal Tribunal found by unanimous decision that Cllr Calver failed to comply with Manorbier Community Council's Code of Conduct, upholding the decision dated 5 November 2010 of the Standards Committee, both as to breach and sanction."

38.   The reasons for the decision are contained in the Panel's decision report, dated 14 July 2011. Its material parts are:

"4.1.5 In relation to breach of paragraph 4(b), the code of conduct applies only when a member is acting in his official capacity. The content of Cllr Calver's website posting or blogs comprised on draft, unapproved, minutes of the Community Council, his opinion and comments about those minutes and about the character and ability of some of the members of the Community Council, the Community Council as a body and how it and certain members conducted themselves. He also alluded to secrecy, connivance, mal-administration, financial mis-management and incompetence and much of this was within his knowledge only because he was an elected member of that authority. He was discussing the affairs and business of his council and his purpose and intention was to inform the people of the community about council or, as he put it, what was going on. Whilst Cllr Calver did not identify himself as the blogger of the owner of the website, those details were easily ascertainable, i.e. that the blogger was Malcolm Calver and that he was a member of that authority. Whilst Cllr Calver says he was not acting in his official capacity, it is an objective test which applies. The Appeal Tribunal concluded that a member of the public reading the website would have the impression, and reasonably so, that Cllr Calver was acting as a member of the Manorbier Community Council.

4.1.6 In relation to paragraph 4(b), having concluded that Cllr Calver was acting in his official capacity, the Appeal Tribunal then considered whether Cllr Calver's posting failed to show respect and consideration for others. The Appeal Tribunal is aware that Cllr Calver asserts that everything he said was true and is aware, from the information before it, of the failings of the Manorbier Community Council. The Appeal Tribunal also notes that Cllr Calver asserts that his motivation was informing the public.

It nevertheless remains the case that Cllr Calver published draft, unapproved minutes after the Community Council had passed a resolution that he should not do so; that he criticised the draft minutes as not being an accurate record of the meeting and the competence of their author; he made personal, snide, remarks about the competence, integrity and character of members of the authority and alluded to alleged breaches by some members of the code of conduct. Whether or not what was said is true does not detract from the rudeness, lack of respect and consideration all of this shows to individual members of the council and the council as a body.

Cllr Calver could have properly addressed his concerns at the next meeting/s thereby allowing others to respond to his views and have their say, allowing a debate and if needs be, a vote. It would have been respectful and considerate for him with the benefit of his experience as a longstanding community and county councillor, to have offered held to those he considered to be less competent and able than himself. Indeed if he was so utterly disgusted with his fellow members on the Community Council, he could have resigned. Instead, he chose to 'bitch from the sidelines' to coin a phrase used by Mr Gwydion Hughes.

4.1.7. Inevitably, the Appeal Tribunal's finding that Cllr Calver has breached the code of conduct by speaking in a way which was inconsiderate and disrespectful to others is, on a superficial level, a breach of his right to freedom of expression under Article 10(1). The Appeal Tribunal does not consider that Cllr Calver's blogs were political expression in the true sense of that meaning; he anonymously blogged on his website by publishing draft unapproved minutes, criticising their content and the competence of their author and made personal comments about the integrity, etc. of the members and the council. It was all very one-sided. It was not an expression of Cllr Calver's political views or allegiances, nor a response to those expressed by others, nor a critique of any other political view or party. The higher level of protection afforded by Article 10(2) to political expression does not apply here therefore. The provisions of the 2008 code of conduct were prescribed by law and the code of conduct is the ethical framework within which local government operates. It sets minimum standards of conduct in public life and upholds those standards of conduct so as to engender public confidence in local democracy. It goes far beyond dealing with corruption; it includes, obviously, a requirement that councillors should treat each other and others with respect and consideration and, as a matter of fact, it is of course perfectly possible to be critical of others without also showing them disrespect or lack of consideration.

4.1.8 Although the Appeal Tribunal has decided that Cllr Calver was acting in his official capacity, it is worth noting that by virtue of paragraph 2(1)(s) the (2008) code of conduct is engaged 'at all times and in any capacity' in respect of conduct identified in paragraph 6(1)(a) (i.e. conduct capable of bringing the office of member or the authority into disrepute.

4.1.9 Cllr Calver was a longstanding and experienced member of the failing Manorbier Community Council; he was also a county councillor. There were various options available to Cllr Calver including seeking to assist those he regarded as incompetent and inexperienced, distancing himself entirely from the failing council by resigning, or seeking the assistance of the monitoring officer. He did none of these. He publicly ridiculed his fellow members and the authority of which he was a member. The Appeal Tribunal conclude that if the reasonable man were asked for his view of Cllr Calver's behaviour, he would say it fell short of that expected, under the code of conduct, of an elected member; and to such extent that it brought his office and his authority into disrepute.

4.1.10 The Appeal Tribunal accordingly decided by unanimous decision to uphold the Standards Committee's determination dated 5 November 2010, that Cllr Calver had breached Manorbier Community Council's code of conduct."

Discussion

39.   It was, subject to one qualification by Mr Hughes, common ground that the questions I must answer are those formulated by Wilkie J in Sanders v Kingston (2005) EWHC 1145 (Admin) at (72). Leaving the qualification to one side at this stage, and adapting Wilkie J's questions to reflect the facts of the present case, they are:

(1) Were the Standards Committee and the Panel entitled as a matter of fact to conclude that the claimant's conduct in respect of the thirteen comments was in breach of paragraphs 4(b) and/or 6(1)(a) of the Code of Conduct?

(2) If so, was the finding in itself or the imposition of a sanction prima facie a breach of Article 10?

(3) If so, was the restriction involved one which was justified by reason of the requirements of Article 10(2)?

40.   Before turning to the application of these questions to the circumstances of the present case, I make five observations about the underlying principles. The first concerns the common law. Understandably, the submissions in this case largely concerned

Article 10 of the Convention. It is, however, important to remember the status of freedom of expression at common law and the relevance of the common law despite the enactment of the Human Rights Act 1998. The continuing importance of common law analysis in this area has been recently illustrated by the decision of the Court of Appeal in R (Guardian News and Media) v City of Westminster Magistrates (2012) EWCA Civ. 420 at (68) per Toulson LJ.

41.   The status of freedom of expression at common law was, for example, seen in the development of the law of defamation and in particular what may be described as the distaste for "prior restraints": Bonnard v Perryman (1891) 2 Ch 269. Its position, although at one stage characterized as a residuary right, has been enhanced by developments of the common law under the influence of rights in international human rights treaties ratified by the United Kingdom, and in particular, even before the Human Rights Act 1998, the European Convention: see Derbyshire CC v Times Newspapers Ltd (1993) AC 554 and R v Secretary of State for the Home Department, ex parte Simms (2000) 2 AC 115, at 126. The result was that a narrower construction was given to legislative instruments restricting the right, and, albeit subject to Parliamentary sovereignty, clear words were required to achieve a restriction. In ex. p. Simms Lord Hoffmann stated (at 131) that "fundamental rights cannot be overridden by general or ambiguous words" because of "the risk that the full implications of their unqualified meaning may have passed unnoticed in the democratic process". See also R (Gillan) v Commissioner of Police for the Metropolis (2006) 2 AC 307 at (15) (per Lord Bingham). This is similar to the position under the Convention. In Jerusalem v Austria (2003) 37 EHRR 25 at (32) the Strasbourg Court stated that the exceptions to freedom of expression must be construed strictly.

42.   Charles J, in R (Mullaney) v Adjudication Panel for England (2009) EWHC 72 (Admin) at (78), expressed no view as to whether, apart from Article 10, a narrow approach should be taken to the

construction of the Code of Practice. But, in McCartan Turkington Green v Times Newspapers (2001) 2 AC 277 at 297 and R v Shayler (2003) 1 AC 247 at (21), Lord Steyn and Lord Bingham respectively described freedom of expression as having "the status of a constitutional right with attendant high normative force", and "a fundamental right" which "has been recognised at common law for very many years". One of the consequences of giving this constitutional status to freedom of expression is that clear words are required to restrict it, and thus in that sense there is a narrower approach to the interpretation of legislation and instruments made under legislation restricting it.

43.   The second observation concerns the approach of the court to the first of Wilkie J's questions. Mr Hughes submitted that the approach and the court's role in this case, a judicial review, is narrower than it is in a statutory appeal such as Sanders v Kingston (2005) EWHC 1145 (Admin). He submitted that, in a judicial review such as this, greater weight should be accorded to the finding of the Panel that the claimant's conduct breached the Code than would be accorded in a statutory appeal. It is true that, in R (Mullaney) v Adjudication Panel for England Charles J referred (at (73) and (74)) to the difference in the role of the court on an appeal under section 79(15) of the 2000 Act from that in a judicial review. It may also in principle be analytically correct to separate the question of whether, in purely common law terms, there is a breach of paragraphs 4(b) or 6(1)(a) of the Code of Conduct from the question of whether there is a breach of Article 10 as questions 1 and 2 do.

44.   I do not, however, consider that those factors affect the conclusion in this case. This is primarily because of the effect of sections 3 and 6 of the Human Rights Act (see (20)) but also because of the approach at common law to restrictions on freedom of expression to which I have referred: see (40) - (42). As far as the common law is concerned, the factors include a cautious approach to the scope of restrictions on it. One manifestation of this is the presumption which (see (41)) prevents rights such as

that to freedom of expression from being overridden by general or ambiguous words. The effect of sections 3 and 6 of the Human Rights Act is that it is in practice difficult entirely to exclude consideration of factors relevant to common law freedom of expression and Article 10 from the question of whether there was a breach of the Code of Conduct. So, for example, in R (Gaunt) v Office of Communications (2011) EWCA Civ 692, Lord Neuberger MR stated (at (36)) that, as it was not contended on behalf of the claimant in that case that the provisions of the Broadcasting Code fell foul of Article 10, they did not require particularly close analysis. However, that did "not alter the fact that the provisions must be interpreted, as well as being applied in a particular case, so as to comply with the requirements of Article 10".

45.   Once Article 10 is under consideration, so is the general approach of the court to questions of weight and latitude in determining whether a decision or conduct is compatible with a Convention right. While (see (73)) the court must "have due regard" to the judgment of the statutory regulator, the approach involves scrutiny of greater intensity than in a judicial review not involving a Convention right, and the decision whether Article 10 is infringed is ultimately one for the court: R (SB) v Governors of Denbigh HS (2007) 1 AC 100 at (30); Belfast City Council v Miss Behavin' Ltd (2007) UKHL 19 at (30), (31) and (88); Gaunt's case at (47). These cases also make it clear that the role of the court is to address the substantive question of compatibility with the Convention right rather than the process used by the primary decision-maker. If, however, the process is defective, less weight will be accorded to the judgment of the primary decision-maker: Belfast City Council v Miss Behavin' Ltd at (37), (47) and (91).

46.   My third observation is that the relevant legal principles in this area do not provide the Panel or the court with bright lines. Notwithstanding the warning by Hoffmann LJ in R v Central Independent Television Plc (1994) 3 All ER 641 at 651-52 they lead it to a process of balancing a number of interests. This is seen, for

example, in Sanders v Kingston at (77) and (84) and in Mullaney's case at (95) – (96) where, in the context of determining whether there was a breach of the Code, Charles J stated that "a balance has to be struck between the various relevant aspects of the public interest in all the circumstances of the case".

47. **As to Hoffmann LJ's warning, he recognised that freedom of expression is subject "to clearly defined exceptions laid down by common law or statute", but did not appear to favour a process of balancing. He stated that, outside those exceptions and any exception enacted in accordance with Parliament's obligations under the Convention, "there is no question of balancing freedom of speech against other interests ... it is a trump card which always wins". That way of putting it may, however, be implicit recognition that, in the approach to and application of those exceptions, there is balancing. Neither freedom of speech nor the principle reflected in the exceptions under consideration (e.g. reputation or privacy) can be given effect in an unqualified way without restricting the other. Hoffmann LJ's concern about balancing was because ((1994) 3 All ER 641, 653) the matters that have to be balanced, in the present case, on one side of the balance a councillor's right to freedom of expression and the public interest in such freedom, and on the other side of the balance the public interest in proper standards of conduct by members of local authorities, are not easily commensurable.**

48.   More recently, in R (Gaunt) v Office of Communications (2011) EWCA Civ 692 at (23) Lord Neuberger MR, considering restrictions on broadcasting "offensive and harmful material" in the Broadcasting Code made pursuant to the Communications Act 2003, stated that "like virtually all human rights, freedom of expression carries with it responsibilities which themselves reflect the power of words, whether spoken or written". Although he also emphasised that "any attempt to curtail freedom of expression must be approached with circumspection", his recognition of the responsibilities that are carried by freedom of expression reflects an

element of balancing. There, of course, has to be balancing when the exercise of the right to free expression in Article 10 right by one person will violate other Convention rights, notably the right to respect for private and family life protected by Article 8.

49.   Fourthly, a process of balancing is, as was recognised in Gaunt's case (at (25)) a highly fact-sensitive one: see also Clayton and Tomlinson, The Law of Human Rights (2nd ed.) 15.297. For this reason, while the cases on the decisions of Case Tribunals and the Adjudication Panel for England to which I have referred (at (8)) provide valuable guidance as to the general approach, it is important to keep in mind their particular facts. Notwithstanding the high importance of freedom of expression and its relative incommensurability with the interests that are invoked in justifying a restriction, the more egregious the conduct, the easier it is likely to be for the Panel, and for the court, to undertake the balancing that is required and justifiably to conclude that what was said or done falls within one of the exceptions to freedom of expression under common law, statute or the Convention. If the conduct is less egregious, it is likely to be more difficult to do this. This is because the interests – freedom of expression and, in the present context, proper standards of conduct by members of local authorities, are not easily commensurable.

50.   Justification requires, as was stated in Livingstone v Adjudication Panel for England (2006) EWHC 2533 (Admin) at (39) "clear and satisfactory reasons within the terms of Article 10(2)". But in Belfast City Council v Miss Behavin' Ltd (2007) UKHL 19 at (92), Lord Neuberger recognised that "it may not always be easy to see, or at least to express in clear terms, how (a person's) Article 10 rights can satisfactorily be weighed against (in that case) a council's decision to refuse a licence".

51.   The conduct found to breach the Code of Conduct in Sanders v Kingston and Mullaney's case was at the top end of the scale of egregiousness. Mullaney's case concerned a Councillor who

trespassed on land to make a video about the condition of a listed building, was involved in a scuffle when the landowner returned, and subsequently uploaded an edited version of the video on the Youtube website. The trespass was a civil wrong (the Councillor also intended to trespass again: (42)) and his involvement in what may have been an affray were undoubtedly serious departures from the standards expected of Councillors established by the framework of the 2000 Act.

52.   Sanders v Kingston involved the response of the claimant, the leader of Peterborough Council, to a request by Carrickfergus Borough Council, a local authority in Northern Ireland. The Carrickfergus Council sought support from English local authorities including the Peterborough Council for its call for an inquiry into the death of a soldier whose family resided in its area and the deaths of other army personnel. Wilkie J described (at (79)) the claimant's initial and later responses to the Carrickfergus Council and to press inquiries as "little more than an expression of personal anger at his time being wasted by (the) request" and (at (81)) "the ill-tempered response of a person who thought that he should not be troubled by the request...and who has chosen to express his annoyance in personal and abusive terms" directed in the main at the Carrickfergus Council and the family of the dead soldier, and as a by-product, the Irish people and "the Troubles". In the present case Mr McCracken QC, on behalf of the claimant, characterized the comments in that case as "not merely offensive but seriously inflammatory" and potentially racist. He noted they caused offence at a national level.

53.   Wilkie J held that the Case Tribunal in that case was fully entitled to find that the conduct did not treat others with respect and was conduct which could reasonably be regarded as bringing the office or authority of the claimant into disrepute. But for the sanction of two years disqualification that was imposed, he would have held the interference with Mr Sanders's freedom of expression was justified in accordance with Article 10(2) of the Convention.

54.   In the present case, before the Panel it was accepted on behalf of the PSOW (see decision report, paragraph 3.2.7) that the conduct in Sanders v Kingston and Gaunt's case (as to which see (56) below) "was atrocious, the worst possible", and very different from the claimant's conduct in this case. But the PSOW's case was that it did not follow that the claimant's conduct did "not fall below that reasonably required by the Code of Conduct". Mr McCracken characterized the claimant's comments in this case as sarcastic, lampooning and disrespectful rather than personal abuse. While it is certainly possible that conduct far less serious than that in those cases can lawfully be found to break the Code of Conduct, it is important not to lose sight of the greater complexity and difficulty for both the Panel and the court in conducting the balancing exercise in such a case.

55.   Fifthly, it is clear, as a general proposition, that freedom of expression includes the right to say things which "right thinking people" consider dangerous or irresponsible or which shock or disturb: see R v Central Independent Television Plc (1994) Fam 192 at 203 (Hoffmann LJ); Redmond-Bates v DPP (1999) 163 JP 789 (Sedley LJ); Jerusalem v Austria (2003) 37 EHRR 25 at (32); Kwiecien v Poland 9 January 2007 (2007) 48 EHRR 7 at (43); Application 27935/05 Filipoviç v Serbia 20 November 2007 at (53). Barendt, Freedom of Speech (2nd ed. 2005) at 76 – 77, in the context of political speech (on which see (58)ff), stated that the exclusion of "all emotive, non-rational expression from the coverage of the principle would be a mistake". It would "often be hard to disentangle such expression from rational discourse" because "the most opprobrious insult may form part of an otherwise serious criticism of government or of a political figure". He also stated that, even if it were possible to separate the emotive content from the other parts of a particular publication, "it would be wrong to allow its proscription" because "if speakers could be punished each time they included a colourful, non-rational epithet in their publication or address, much valuable

speech would be inhibited". He concluded that "some margin should be allowed for invective and exaggeration, even if that means some apparently worthless comments are as fully protected as a carefully balanced argument". The statements of Hoffmann LJ in the Central Independent Television case that "a freedom which is restricted to what judges think to be responsible or in the public interest is no freedom" and that freedom of expression means "the right to publish things which government and judges, however well motivated, think should not be published" and of Sedley LJ in Redmond-Bates v DPP that "freedom only to speak inoffensively is not worth having", are clearly relevant and have been relied on by courts considering restrictions in codes made pursuant to statutory authority.

56.   For example, in Livingstone v Adjudication Panel for England (2006) EWHC 2533 (Admin), Collins J, considering the Code of Conduct of the Greater London Authority, and referring to **Hoffmann LJ's observations in the Central Independent Television case, stated (at (36)) that "surprising as it may perhaps appear to some, the right of freedom of speech does extend to abuse".** See also Sanders v Kingston (2005) EWHC 1145 (Admin) at (77) and the approach of the Court of Appeal in R (Gaunt) v Office of Communications (2011) EWCA Civ 692 at (27) – (29). In Gaunt's case Ofcom had found that a radio interview violated the Broadcasting Code. The Court of Appeal referred to Sedley LJ's statement in the Richmond-Bates case. But, notwithstanding that and the strength of the right to freedom of expression, the extremely aggressive tone of the interviewer, the constant interruptions, insults, ranting and the lack of any substantive content led it to conclude that Ofcom had correctly concluded the interviewer had broken the relevant provisions of the Broadcasting Code, and that neither the Code nor its application in that case fell foul of Article 10.

57.   Although the fact-sensitive approach (see (49)) means there is no rigid typology of forms of expression (see Clayton and Tomlinson, The Law of Human Rights 2nd ed. 15.297), it has also

been said that "the value of free speech in a particular case must be measured in specifics" and that "not all types of speech have an equal value": Lord Steyn in R v Secretary of State for the Home Department, ex. p Simms (1999) 3 All ER 400 at 408. See also R (Gaunt) v Office of Communications (2011) EWCA Civ 692 at (25) per Lord Neuberger MR. In Jerusalem v Austria (2003) 37 EHRR 25 at (35) it was stated that in examining the particular circumstances of the case, the Court will take the following into account: the position of the applicant who complains that his right to freedom of expression under Article 10 has been violated, the position of the person or institution which has done so, and the subject-matter of the words or conduct about which the complaint is made.

58.   The gradations in the value of free speech also mean that the statements **by Hoffmann and Sedley LJJ I have quoted at (55) are particularly relevant in the present context. This is because of the recognition of the importance of expression in the political sphere and that the limits of acceptable criticism are wider in the case of politicians acting in their public capacity than they are in the case of private individuals: see Jerusalem v Austria at (36). This recognition involves both a higher level of protection ("enhanced protection") for statements in the political sphere and the expectation that if the subjects of such statements are politicians acting in their public capacity, they lay themselves open to close scrutiny of their words and deeds and are expected to possess a thicker skin and greater tolerance than ordinary members of the public: see Jerusalem v Austria at (38), albeit referring to what journalists and the public say about politicians, and, in a common law context, Lange v Australian Broadcasting Corp. (1997) 189 CLR 520, 559 (High Court of Australia). Although the protection of Article 10(2) extends to politicians, the Strasbourg Court has stated that where a politician seeks to rely on it, "the requirements have to be weighed in relation to the open discussion of political issues": Lingens v Austria (1986) 8 EHRR 103 at (42).**

59.   Mr Hughes submitted (skeleton argument, paragraph 28) that within the category of political speech there are also gradations, and that the "level of political debate that takes place at a Community Council level ought to be less heated and contentious" than debate at the national level. But, whether or not this is so, it is clear, as Mr Hughes also recognised, that political expression at local council level also attracts enhanced protection. **In Jerusalem v Austria, whether or not the debate in the Vienna Municipal Council occurred when the Council was sitting as a local authority rather than as the Land (State) Parliament (which it also was), the Strasbourg court stated (at (40)) that "very weighty reasons must be advanced to justify interfering with the freedom of expression exercised therein".**

60.   **There may be a difference between manifestations of freedom of expression during a meeting of the Council and such manifestations outside such meetings (see Sanders v Kingston at (77) and (85)) but the enhanced protection can apply whether or not the conduct occurs during such a meeting.** So, in Filipoviç v Serbia 20 November 2007, a statement by Mr Filipoviç at a public meeting in a municipal hall that a mayor was guilty of embezzlement attracted the enhanced protection. The meeting was attended by two Deputy Ministers, some eighty local councillors and other leading local figures. Its purpose (see judgment at (15)) was to assess the functioning of the municipality as a whole and those attending were encouraged to share their "critical views". The statement could not be regarded as one of fact and indeed (see judgment at (54)) it was not corroborated by any relevant evidence. See also Kwiecien v Poland (2007) 48 EHRR 7 at (43), in relation to an open letter distributed in a period preceding an election alleging that the Head of District Office who was seeking election carried out duties ineptly and in breach of the law.

61.   This does not mean that everything said by a politician or a member of a local council will attract enhanced protection. I have referred (see (52)) to the way Wilkie J characterized what Councillor

Sanders said in Sanders v Kingston. Wilkie J stated (at (79)) that there was nothing in what the Case Tribunal found that Councillor Sanders wrote and said "which could properly be described as political expression of views". In Livingstone's case, the then Mayor of London's words were addressed to a Jewish journalist employed by the Daily Mail, a newspaper which the then Mayor considered had persecuted him and was part of a group which he considered (see (2006) EWHC 2533 (Admin) at (8)) had a past record of pre-war support for anti-Semitism and Nazism and what he regarded as its continuing racist bigotry, hatred and prejudice. Mr Livingstone asked the journalist whether he was a German war criminal, and stated inter alia that he "was just like a concentration camp guard". Collins J (see (36)) had no doubt that the then Mayor was "not to be regarded as expressing a political opinion which attracts the high level of protection" but "indulging in offensive abuse of a journalist whom he regarded as carrying out on his newspaper's behalf activities which (he) regarded as abhorrent".

62. So, how is the line to be drawn? Mr McCracken submitted that sarcasm and lampooning of those who have placed themselves in public office falls within the enhanced protection. He also maintained there should be no sharp distinction between national and local governmental bodies. He relied on the definition from Collins' Dictionary of the English Language; "of or relating to the state, government, the body politic, public administration, policy, etc", the speech of Baroness Hale in Campbell v Mirror Group Newspapers (2004) 2 AC 457 at (148) – (149), and the etymology of the word from the Greek work for city. He relied on etymology in support of his submission that it is clear that the relevant unit of government may be a local one rather than a country but, since ancient Greece consisted of many more or less independent city-states, etymology is of limited assistance in respect of this particular point.

63. Hare's contribution to a collection of essays in honour of Sir David Williams observes that beyond obvious illustrations, there are

difficulties in defining political expression, and that the variety of formulations in different contexts should "make us hesitate before adopting a view of the importance of political expression which will inevitably lead to further litigation surrounding the definition of its organising concept": Freedom of Expression and Freedom of Information (OUP 2000), at 108 and 112. In the context of Article 10, Baroness Hale, in Campbell v Mirror Group Newspapers, included the following within the category of political speech:

"...information on matters relevant to the organisation of the economic, social and political life of the country".

This, she stated, included "revealing information about public figures, especially those in elective office, which would otherwise be private but is relevant to their participation in public life". This is consistent with what was stated in an entirely different context by Lord Hardwicke. In Chesterfield v Janssen (1751) 2 Ves. Sen. 125, at 156; 28 English Reports at 100, he stated that politics "comprehends everything that concerns the government of the country, of which the administration of justice makes a considerable part".

64.   As to the breadth of the concept of political expression in the Strasbourg jurisprudence, in Thorgeirson v Iceland (1992) 14 EHRR 843 at (64) (in the context of a complaint by a journalist that criminal defamation proceedings in respect of articles alleging brutality by a police force violated his rights under Article 10) the Court stated:

"there is no warrant in its case law for distinguishing ... between political discussion and discussion of other matters of public concern."

It is in this sense that the statement by Clayton and Tomlinson, 15.284 that "the concept of political expression is broadly interpreted" should be understood. See also Barendt, Freedom of Speech (2nd ed. 2005) who, at 154, refers to "speech in the political sphere", at 159 to "speech on matters of public concern", and the passages from 76 – 77 quoted at (55). See also the cases to which I have referred at (60).

65.   I turn to the application of these principles and factors to the circumstances of the present case and the questions identified by Wilkie J in Sanders v Kingston. I have referred (see (43) – (45)) to the difficulty in excluding common law freedom of expression and Article 10 factors from the question of whether the Standards Committee and the Panel were entitled as a matter of fact to conclude that the claimant's conduct in respect of the thirteen comments was in breach of paragraphs 4(b) and/or 6(1)(a) of the Code of Conduct. However, for present purposes, as a pure matter of language, and without regard at this stage to my obligation under section 3 of the Human Rights Act to interpret the Code so far as it is possible so as to comply with the requirements of Article 10, I have done so. I shall return to the impact of common law and Convention principles on instruments which affect freedom of expression.

66.   Approaching the first of the questions identified in Sanders v Kingston in this way, I have concluded that the Committee and the Panel were entitled to conclude that the thirteen comments by the claimant breached the Code. First, whether or not it is accurate to characterise the comments as "snide", they were, as Mr McCracken accepted, sarcastic and mocking. Secondly, the Panel was entitled to take a cumulative view of the effect of the claimant's postings. In this respect the conduct which has led to the finding of breach and the sanction in this case differs from the conduct in Livingstone and Mullaney. Sanders's case, of course, involved a course of conduct, albeit over a shorter period. Disregarding Article 10 and section 3 of the Human Rights Act, the use of a sarcastic tone about colleagues on the Council over a long period would justify a conclusion that the claimant had not shown respect and consideration for his colleagues on the Council.

67.   Thirdly, the Panel was entitled to conclude that the tone of the claimant's postings "publicly ridiculed his fellow members", particularly in the light of the number of postings and their

cumulative effect. The juxta positioning in different postings of the criticisms of the quality and accuracy of the minutes produced by Cllr Gourlay and the comments about the fact that she had not been elected in a contested ballot (comment (3) and possibly comment (13)), and comment (5) on declarations of interest do make it appear that the comments were intended to undermine her in an unattractive way. Her letter dated 3 March 2009 to the PSOW shows she felt she had been subjected to intense ridicule. These comments and a number of the others could be characterized, as the PSOW did in his submissions to the Panel (decision report, paragraph 3.26) as "snide comments, remarks of a general derogatory nature in a sarcastic tone". I do not, however, accept Mr Hughes's submission that the comments on the blog which were found to breach the Code of Conduct challenged the mental capacity of other Councillors. The nearest to this is comment (1) stating that the Council "did not understand the limits of its role". But that is an allegation of a defect of a different order.

68.   As to the criticism that the Panel also took into account ridicule of the Council itself, I accept Mr Hughes' submission that, looking at the ruling as whole, notwithstanding the reference to ridicule of "the authority" and "the Council as a body" in paragraphs 4.1.6 and 4.1.9 of the decision report, it was the fact that the claimant's comments were directed at his fellow members that was the heart of the Panel's findings.

69.   The Standards Committee and the Panel found that twelve of the thirteen comments breached paragraph 6(1)(a) which applies at all times to a member of a Council whether or not he or she is acting, claiming to act, or giving the impression of acting in the role of Council member It was thus only in respect of comment (5) where the only breach found is of paragraph 4(b) that it was necessary to find that the claimant was so acting, although there were five other comments where breaches of both paragraphs were found. The Panel was entitled to conclude that the claimant was acting in his capacity as a member of the Community Council in

respect of comment (5) and the five comments which were found to breach both paragraphs. The claimant's evidence is that "during both terms of my office (I have) provided information on the website of decisions, comments etc of what goes on at Council meetings and what currently and previously has been hidden from both public and Council/Councillors alike". I do not accept the claimant's contention that, because none of the information was confidential to him as a Councillor, his position as a Councillor did not preclude him from speaking out "as a citizen". Whether or not the information was confidential, some of it was only available to the claimant because of his position, although (see Mullaney's case at (85(i)) this is not a requirement. Moreover, it was his principal way of communicating with his constituents and others in the community, and the content of his blog was almost exclusively the business of the Community Council.

70.   Mr McCracken submitted (skeleton argument, paragraph 45) that in some contexts, where criticism is the performance of a duty, "the concept of 'rudeness' has no place and that it was as absurd for the Panel to condemn a politician for 'rudeness' in his sincere criticism of the shortcomings of fellow politicians as it would be to criticise a judge for the offensive nature of his remarks in sentencing a criminal". He also submitted (skeleton argument, paragraphs 40, 42 and 47) that, since nearly all the comments were true and reflected the past and present failings in the administration of the council's business, it was those whose actions were reported who brought the council and the office of councillor into disrepute. I reject these submissions. I have concluded that in principle this regular conduct over such a long period did prima facie bring the claimant's office into disrepute.

71.   I turn to the second and third questions identified in Sanders v Kingston. The submissions by both parties focused on the position under the Convention and the remainder of this judgment will also do so. Mr Hughes accepted that the finding was prima facie a breach of the claimant's right to freedom of expression and of

Article 10. It is not arguable that the legislative scheme making provision for Codes of Conduct for Councillors or the Codes of Conduct made under the 2000 Act are too uncertain to qualify as being prescribed by law: see Sanders v Kingston at (61) and (84) and Mullaney's case at (70). Accordingly, the real issue concerns the third question, whether the restriction was one which was justified by reason of the requirements of (and the application of the factors in) Article 10(2) and I turn to that.

72.   In these proceedings it has not been necessary to consider the distinction in the Strasbourg jurisprudence between facts and value judgments (on which, see Clayton and Tomlinson, The Law of Human Rights (2nd ed.) 15.314 -315) because the Panel's conclusions proceed on the basis that what was said in the claimant's comments was true. It stated in paragraph 4.16 that "whether or not what was said is true does not detract from the rudeness, lack of respect and consideration" the claimant's comments showed to individual members of the Council and the Council as a body. It suffices to say that restrictions on publication of both matters which are factual in nature and are demonstrated to be true, and of value judgments are generally difficult to justify under Article 10(2).

73.   **It is common ground that the court, in considering whether the Panel failed to accord sufficient weight to the claimant's rights to freedom of expression, has to decide for itself whether those rights were accorded sufficient weight, having due regard to the decision of the Panel.** The court must "have due regard" to the judgment of the primary decision-maker, in this case the Panel. This is because the Panel, the statutory regulator, consists of persons identified by Parliament to apply the Code because of its knowledge and experience of local government: Mullaney's case at (72); Gaunt's case at (47); Belfast City Council v Miss-Behavin' Ltd (2007) UKHL 19 at (26), (37) and (46). But "due regard" does not mean that the process is only one of review: **it is the court which has to decide whether the Panel has violated the claimant's right to**

freedom of expression.

74.   The Code seeks to maintain standards and to ensure that the conduct of public life at the local government level, including political debate, does not fall below a minimum level so as (see decision report, paragraph 4.1.7) "to engender public confidence in local democracy". Mr Hughes submitted (skeleton argument, paragraph 34) that it seeks to ensure that it does not descend to the level of personal abuse and ridicule "because when debate and public life is conducted at the level of personal abuse and ridicule, the public loses confidence in it and those involved in it". There is a clear public interest in maintaining confidence in local government. **But in assessing what conduct should be proscribed and the extent to which sarcasm and ridicule should be, it is necessary to bear in mind the importance of freedom of political expression or speech in the political sphere in the sense I have stated (at (58) – (64)) it has been used in the Strasbourg jurisprudence.**

75.   The fact that more candidates did not come forward at the 2008 election to the Community Council may have reflected the disenchantment of local residents with the Council and loss of confidence in it. That may have been the result of the difficulties which I summarised at (22) – (25) and which led it to be described as a failing Council. It may also in part have been the result of the way the relationships between Councillors had been perceived by those who lived in the Community. Against that background, it is certainly understandable that the Monitoring Officer, the Standards Committee and the Panel were concerned about what was going on in this particular Community Council. It is of some significance that, as well as requiring the claimant to be re-trained as to the requirements of the Code of Conduct, the Standards Committee in this case recommended that other Councillors be re-trained.

76.   **It is in the context of what constitutes "respect and consideration" and "bringing your office or authority into disrepute" in a local government context that the Panel's**

expertise is of particular relevance. Because of this I have given most anxious consideration to the conclusion that I was minded to reach after considering the oral and written submissions. After doing so, I have nevertheless decided that the Panel fell into error in a number of respects.

77.   **The first and most important concerns its approach to "political expression".** Mr Hughes submitted that the Panel and the Standards Committee were correct in finding that the comments found to breach the Code were not expressions of political views because they had "nothing to do with political debate or political views" although, had they related to "political policy or political competence" they might have attracted the enhanced standard of protection: skeleton argument, paragraphs 31 and 29. In his oral submissions, he accepted that some of the comments were either "political" (comment (4)) or "close to political" (comment (1). Although Mr Hughes's oral submissions focused on the contention that the criticisms of the minutes were criticisms of the literacy of the minute-taker, comments (2), and (11) were (as he recognised in his skeleton argument, paragraphs 29 and 31), concerned with their quality, accuracy, and availability.

78.   **The Panel in paragraph 4.1.7 of the decision report states that it did not consider that the blogs were political expression "in the true sense of that meaning". The factors referred to by the Panel included that "it was all very one-sided". That does not, however, preclude something being political expression: indeed, some would say that it is a feature of much political expression.**

79.   The Panel also stated that the comments were "not an expression of Cllr Calver's political views or allegiances, nor a response to those expressed by others, nor a critique of any other political view of party" and that the higher level of protection "does not apply here therefore". But the statements in Filipoviç v Serbia 20 November 2007 (mayor guilty of embezzlement) and in Kwiecien v Poland 9 January 2007 (2007) 48 EHRR 7 (head of local authority

carried out duties ineptly and in breach of the law) are also not expressions of or critiques of political views.

80.   I have concluded that the Panel took an over-narrow view of what amounts to "political expression" (see the authorities discussed at (57) – (64) above) and that, taken in the round, so have the submissions of Mr Hughes on this point. Not all of the claimant's comments were political expression even in the broad sense the term has been used in this context. It is, for example, difficult to see how comments (3) and (5) qualify, and comment (12) must at best be on the borderline. I have described the comments as sarcastic and mocking, and some as seeking to undermine Cllr Gourlay in an unattractive way. However, notwithstanding what I have said about their tone, the majority relate to the way the Council meetings were run and recorded. Some of them were about the competence of Cllr Gourlay who, albeit in a voluntary capacity in the absence of a Council official, was taking the minutes and no doubt trying to do her best. Others were about the provision of minutes to Councillors or the approach of Councillors to declarations of interest. The comments were in no sense "high" manifestations of political expression. But, they (or many of them) were comments about the inadequate performance of Councillors in their public duties. As such, in my judgment, they fall within the term "political expression" in the broader sense the term has been applied in the Strasbourg jurisprudence. For the reasons given at (55), it is difficult to disentangle the sarcasm and mockery from the criticism of the way Council meetings were run.

1.   *Secondly, although the essence of the framework set out by the 2000 Act and the Code of *Conduct is to restrict the conduct of Councillors not only vis a vis the public and staff but *including that towards colleagues on the Council, no account was taken in the Panel's *decision of what is said in the Strasbourg jurisprudence about the need for politicians to have *thicker skins than others.

82.   *The fact that the Panel took a narrower view of "political expression" and did not refer to the *need for politicians to have thicker skins than others limits the weight that can be given to its *findings: see (45) above and Belfast City Council v Miss Behavin' Ltd. It thus falls to the court to determine whether the restriction in this case was a disproportionate interference with the claimant's right to freedom of expression without the assistance of the Panel on these questions and accordingly the Panel's decision has less weight than it otherwise would have.

83.   *The requirement of "necessity in a democratic society" in Article 10(2) sets a high threshold. *It was made clear in R v Shayler (2003) 1 AC 247 at (23) by Lord Bingham of Cornhill (citing *language used in Strasbourg cases such as Handyside v United Kingdom (1976) 1 EHRR *737 at (48)) that the concept is less flexible than expressions such as "reasonable" or *"desirable". As to proportionality, in Shayler's case, Lord Hope stated (at (61)) that those *seeking to justify a restriction must establish that "the means used impair the right as *minimally as possible". In Sanders v Kingston Wilkie J recognised that, in the context of *political debate, there may be robust and even offensive statements in respect of which a *finding that the Code had been breached would be an unlawful infringement of the rights *protected by Article 10 (see (2005) EWHC 1145 (Admin at (77) and (85)) although he found *that was not such a case.

84.   Despite the unattractiveness of much of what was posted, most of it was not purely personal abuse of the kind seen in Livingstone's case. It did not involve a breach of obligation, as the conduct in Mullaney's case did. Nor does it come close in kind or degree of condemnation to the language which has been held to be "unparliamentary" by the Speaker of the House of Commons. I accept Mr McCracken's submission that it is necessary to bear in mind the traditions of robust debate, which may include some degree of lampooning of those who place themselves in public office, when deciding what constitutes the "respect and

consideration" required by the Code. I have concluded that, in the light of the strength of the right to freedom of expression, particularly in the present context, and the fact that the majority of the comments posted were directed at other members of the Community Council, the Panel's decision that they broke the Code is a disproportionate interference with the claimant's rights under Article 10 of the Convention.

85.   At this stage it is necessary to return to the construction of the Code of conduct, but now taking account of the common law and Convention positions on freedom of expression. In Mullaney's case Charles J described the concepts of "respect" and "acting in an official capacity" as having a chameleon quality dependent on context: (2009) EWHC 72 (Admin) at (70). He stated (at (78)) that, because of Article 10, a narrow approach should be taken to the construction of the Code of Practice. Words and phrases such as "respect", "consideration", and "bringing office or authority into disrepute" must be construed in the light of that. Given the "chameleon" or open-textured quality of these terms, and the recognition (see (42)) that at common law freedom of expression has "the status of a constitutional right with attendant high normative force", in principle a common law narrow construction of the provisions of the Code in accordance with the statement from Lord Hoffmann's speech in ex p Simms set out at (41) may well mean that the majority of the thirteen comments do not breach paragraphs 4(b) and 6(1)(a). But if it does not, I consider that it is possible to read and give effect to those provisions of the Code in a Convention compatible way. If so, section 3 of the Human Rights Act obliges me and the Panel to do so.

86.   I deal briefly with a number of subsidiary matters. The Panel took into account what it considered were the alternative options open to the claimant. Paragraph 4.1.9, however, wrongly suggested that the claimant had not sought the assistance of the Monitoring Officer. He had in fact done this in relation to the minutes. Also, albeit much earlier, in 2006, he had sought to deal with his concerns about the Council by complaining to the PSOW. He was,

however, told (see (23)) that the matter fell outside the PSOW's remit. Secondly, I am somewhat troubled by the Panel's reference to resignation as an option available to the claimant if he was "so utterly disgusted" with his fellow Councillors. In respect of the deficiencies in the administrative arrangements concerning declarations of interest and minute-taking at a local representative body which were concerning the claimant, this comes close to a suggestion that one must put up or get out.

87.   I also note that in paragraph 4.1.7 of the decision report, in the context of considering whether the comments amounted to political expression, the Panel took into account the publication of the draft unapproved minutes and what are described as personal comments about the "integrity" of the members and the Council. The Standards Committee had, however, not accepted that the publication of the draft minutes breached the Code or that the claimant had made comments about the "integrity" of the members and the Council.

88.   As to the sanction, this was at the lower end of the sanctions that the Panel could impose Had the interference been otherwise justified, I would not have been minded to hold that the sanction imposed itself meant the decision was a disproportionate interference with the claimant's rights under Article 10. I, however, note that the Panel could have simply imposed a requirement of further training without censuring the claimant or found a breach but taken no further action. Albeit in respect of what might well have been a very different factual scenario, that is (see (30)) what the Standards Committee did in respect of the claimant's complaints about Cllr Hughes' failures in respect of declarations of interest. Although the Standards Committee found Cllr Hughes had breached the Code, it recommended that no further action should be taken.

89.   *In view of my conclusions, it is not strictly necessary to consider the two subsidiary issues to *which I referred at (5). I

very much doubt that the fact that the claimant signed a *declaration consenting to be bound by the provisions of the Code can make a *difference, because he was required by statute so to sign. It cannot be inferred from *that statutory requirement that he was required to consent to a Code which included *provisions for determinations which would disproportionately restrict his Article 10 *rights. Since the Code of Conduct can and must be interpreted so as to give effect to *Article 10 rights, the question of whether the Code itself is ultra vires, which was *raised contingently by Mr McCracken, does not arise.

90.   For the reasons I have given, the claimant's application is granted and the Panel's decision must be set aside.

THE RULES OF NATURAL JUSTICE

A checklist

No one who even appears to have any reason at all to prejudge the outcome should take part in the decision-making.

The same person should not act as accuser, prosecutor, judge and jury.

No one should be tried in his or her absence
No one should be tried who has not been given notice of the charges against him or her.
Everyone should see all the documents to be relied on.
Everyone should have adequate time to prepare his or her case or defence
Everyone should have an opportunity to test the evidence and question any witnesses brought by the other side.

Mr Justice Megarry, from Hansard.

"We have all known cases which appeared to be open and shut, and were not. We have all known arguments which appeared to be unanswerable, and were not. We have all known determinations which appeared to be unshakeable, and were changed by argument".

"Nemo iudex. The 'bias' rule: no one may be judge in his own case.

Audi alteram partem. **The rule that both sides of the case should be heard**

Statutory power: Duty not to act 'ultra vires'.

HTV Ltd v Price Commission (1976) Lord Denning - Master of the Rolls "A public body which is entrusted by Parliament with the exercise of powers for the public good cannot fetter itself in the exercise of them. It cannot be estopped from doing its public duty. **But that is subject to the qualification that it must not misuse its powers: and it is a misuse of power for it to act unfairly or unjustly towards a private citizen when there is no overriding public interest to warrant it ".**

Natural Justice

A. Definition

Natural Justice is an umbrella term for the legal standards of basic fairness. It is a fundamental doctrine within the common law, rested in centuries of legal tradition.

R v Panel on Takeovers and Mergers, ex parte Datafin PLC (1987). Sir John Donaldson, Master of the Rolls

"... a failure to observe the basic rules of natural justice, which is probably better described as fundamental unfairness since justice in nature is conspicuous by its absence."

B.   **Importance**

John v Rees (1970) .
Justice Megarry

"It may be that there are some who would decry the importance of the rules of natural justice. ......those who take this view do not, I think, do themselves justice. As everybody who has anything to do with the law well knows, the path of the law is strewn with examples of open and shut cases which, somehow, were not: of unanswerable charges which, in the event, were completely answered ; with inexplainable conduct which was fully explained; .... nor are those with any knowledge of human nature who pause to think for a moment likely to underestimate the feelings of resentment of those who find there is a decison against them as being made without their being afforded any opportunity to influence the course of events."

C.   Parliament's Intent

Fairmount Investments Ltd v Secretary of State for the Environment (1976) Lord Russell

"I am satisfied that if the true conclusion is that the course which events followed resulted in that degree of unfairness ... that it is commonly referred to as a departure from the principles of natural justice and it may equally be said that the order is not within the powers of the Act and that a requirement of the Act has not been complied with. For it is to be implied, unless the contrary appears, that Parliament does not authorise by the Act the exercise of powers in breach of the principles of natural justice, and that Parliament does by the Act require, in particular procedures, compliance with those principles ."

R v Commission for Racial Equality ex parte Hillingdon London Borough Council (1982) - Lord Diplock

"I do not think that in administrative law as it has developed over the last 20 years attaching a label 'quasi-judicial' to it is of any significance.   Where an Act of Parliament confers upon an administrative body functions which involves making decisions which affect to their detriment the rights of other persons ... there is a presumption that Parliament intended that the administrative

body should act fairly towards those persons who will be affected by their decision."
R v Tower Hamlets London Borough Council ex parte Chetnik Developments Ltd (1988) Lord Bridge

"Statutory power conferred for public purposes is conferred as if it were upon trust, not absolutely - that is to say, it can validly be used only in the right and proper way in which Parliament when conferring it is presumed to have intended."

R v Secretary of State for Foreign and Commonwealth Affairs, ex parte World Development Movement Ltd (1995)
Lord Justice Rose

"statutory powers however permissive, must be used with scrupulous attention to their true purposes and for reasons which are relevant and proper"

Lord Steyn (1997)

"We live in a democracy in the narrow sense that majority rule prevails but, more importantly, we live in a liberal European democracy based on values of justice, liberty, equality and humanity. Judges are therefore entitled to assume, unless the Statute makes crystal clear provision to the contrary, that Parliament would not wish to make unjust laws."

R v Secretary of State for the Home Department ex parte Pierson (1998) Lord Steyn

"... unless there is the clearest provision to the contrary, Parliament must be presumed not to legislate contrary to the rule of law. And the rule of law enforces minimum standards of fairness, both substantive and procedural."

R v Secretary of State for the Environment Transport & the Regions ex p Spath Holme (2001) Lord Nicholls

"No statutory power is of unlimited scope"

D.   Rights and Duties

1) Duty to promote the legislative purpose

R v Secretary of State for Home Department ex parte
Brind (1991)   Lord Ackner

"The discretion .... must be used only to advance the purposes
for which it was conferred.   It has accordingly to be used to
promote the policy and objects of the Act."

2) Duty not to act 'ultra vires'

HTV Ltd v Price Commission (1976)
Lord Denning - Master of the Rolls

"A public body which is entrusted by Parliament with the exercise
of powers for the public good cannot fetter itself in the exercise of
them. It cannot be estopped from   doing its public duty. But that
is subject to the qualification that it must not misuse its powers:
and it is a misuse of power for it to act unfairly or unjustly towards a
private citizen when there is no overriding public interest to warrant
it".

Bromley London Borough Council v Greater London
Council (1983)   Lord Scarman

"The unreasonableness of the decision i.e. that which would enable
the Court to conclude that it is one which no reasonable authority
could have reached, is that it proceeded upon a misconception of
the duties imposed upon the appellants by the statute."

R v Hendon Justices, ex parte Director of Public Prosecutions (1994)

"It is implicit in the enactment that a conferred power is not to be exercised unreasonably ………. If it is ... the conferred power can be characterized as illegal, void or a nullity"

3) Duty to act in good faith
Board of Education v Rice 1911   Lord Loreburn

"They must act in good faith and fairly listen to both sides, for that is the duty lying upon everyone who decides anything".

4) Duty to act reasonable

Roberts v Hopwood 1925   Lord Wrenbury

"A person in whom is vested a discretion must exercise his discretion upon reasonable grounds. A discretion does not empower a man to do what he likes merely because he is minded to do so - he must generally exercise the discretion to do not what he likes but what he ought. In other words, he must, by use of his reason, ascertain and follow the course which reason directs. He must act reasonably"

R v Department for Education & Employment ex parte Begbie(2000)   Lord Justice Laws

"Fairness and reasonableness and their contraries are objective concepts: otherwise there would be no public law, or if there were it would be palm tree justice."

5) Right to fairness

Bushell v Secretary of State for the Environment (1981) Lord Diplock

"in exercising their discretion, as in exercising any other administrative function they owe a constitutional duty to perform it fairly and honestly and to the best of their ability"
Board of Education of the Indian Head School Division of 19 of Saskatchewan v Knight (1990)

" The existence of a general duty to act fairly will depend on the consideration of three factors:

i)   The nature of the decision to be made by the administrative body
ii) The relationship existing between that body and the individual
iii) The effect of that decision on the individual's right"

R v Inland Revenue Commissioners ex parte Unilever PLC (1996)   Lord Justice Simon Brown

"Unfairness amounting to an abuse of power .... it is unlawful .... because it is illogical or immoral or both for a public authority to act with conspicuous unfairness and in that sense abuse its power".

R v Secretary of State for Home Department ex parte Pierson (1998)   Lord Hope

Referring to the Secretary of State as " bound by considerations of substantive unfairness ...... as there are no statutory rules, the presumption must be that he will exercise his powers in a manner which is fair in all the circumstances."

6) **Right to procedural fairness**

Greater London Council (1985)

Lord Justice Muskill

Went on to identify four ways in which a decision might be procedurally improper, namely,

    1.   Unfair behaviour towards persons affected by the decision.

    2.   Failure to follow a procedure laid down by legislation.

3.   Failure properly to marshall the evidence on which the decision should be based. For example taking into account an immaterial factor or failing to take into account a material factor or failing to take reasonable steps to obtain the relevant information.

4.   Failure to approach the decision in the right spirit for example where the decision maker is actuated by bias or where he is content to let the decision be made by chance"

7) Duty of enquiry

The Secretary of State for Education and Science v Tameside M B C (1977)   Lord Diplock.

"the question for the Court is did the Secretary of State ask himself the right question and take reasonable steps to acquaint himself with the relevant information to enable him to answer it correctly?"

R v Secretary of State for the Home Department ex parte Venables (1998)   Lord Justice Hobhouse

"Essential that (the Secretary of State) should be fully informed of all material facts and circumstances", "it is not clear what account the Secretary of State took of this consideration nor that he took any steps to inform himself of the relevant facts",

8) Duty to ask the right question

Secretary of State for Education and Science v

Tameside M B C (1977)   Lord Wilberforce

"The ultimate question in this case, in my opinion, is whether the Secretary of State has given sufficient, or any, weight to this particular factor in the exercise of his judgement."

Lord Diplock

"The Secretary of State did not direct his mind to the right question; and so, since his good faith is not in question, he cannot have directed himself properly in law"

9) Duty to consider all relevant material

R v Secretary of State for the Home Department ex parte Nelson (1994)

"Not satisfied that the material before the Secretary of State was properly considered before the decision was taken"

R v Legal Aid Area Number 1 (London) Appeal Committee ex parte McCormick (2000)

"The Committee cannot simply leave those issues in the air since their resolution ... could be beneficial ...", "serious doubts about whether they did take into consideration all potentially relevant factors"

10) Duty to consider relevant evidence

Dakar v Minister of Transport

"There may be situations when the Ministerial body has not taken any extraneous factors into account and has confined itself solely to relevant factors, yet there has been such a distortion and lack of proportion given to the weight given to these that the final result cannot possibly hold up and is therefore, completely unreasonable."

> Secretary of State for Education & Science v Tameside Metropolitan Borough
> Council (1977) Lord Wilberforce

"The ultimate question in this case, in my opinion, is whether the Secretary of State has given sufficient, or any, weight to this particular factor in the exercise of his judgement"

Recommendation Number R (80)2 of the Committee of Ministers (adopted 11 March   (1980)

In describing this basic principle "an administrative authority when exercising a discretionary power ………. observes objectivity and impartiality, taking into account any of the factors relevant to the particular case".

> R v Parliamentary Commissioner for Administration, ex parte Balchin (1998)

"The relevant test ………. as well as a consideration has been omitted which, had account been taken of it, might have caused the decision maker to reach a different conclusion"

> R v Director General of Telecommunications, ex parte Cellcom Ltd (1999)   Justice Lightman
>
> > "The Court may interfere if the Director has taken into account an irrelevant consideration or has failed to take into account a relevant consideration."

R (on the application of Alconbury Developments Ltd) v Secretary of State for the Environment and the Regions (2001) Lord Slynn

"It has long been established that if the Secretary of State .... takes into account matters irrelevant to his decision or refuses or fails to take into account matters relevant to his decision .... The Court may set his decision aside".

11) Duty to consider evidence of probative value

Mahon v Air New Zealand Ltd (1984) Lord Diplock

In referring to a principle of natural justice that an investigative decision maker "must base his decision upon evidence that has some probative value."

R v Wakefield Magistrates Court ex parte Wakefield M B C (2000)

The Magistrates decision "fatally flawed by its error of law in purporting to make a critical finding of fact, without having heard any evidence called in the proceedings upon which that finding of fact could properly be founded"

12) A right to see documents relied on
T A Miller v Ministry of Housing Local Government (1968)

"The person at risk should have an opportunity to comment on materials being considered by the decision maker and to contradict them".

Wiseman v Borneman (1971) Lord Morris

"I feel bound to express my prima facie dislike of a situation in which the tribunal has before it a document (which might contain both facts and arguments) which was calculated to influence the tribunal but which has not been seen by a party who will be affected by the tribunal's decision"

Lord Wilberforce

"The natural aversion against allowing a decision to be made on the basis of material he has not seen"

R v London Borough of Camden ex parte Paddock
(1995)   Justice Sedley

"The principle that a decision making body should not see relevant to giving those affected the chance to comment on it and if they wish, to controvert it is fundamental to the principle of law (which governs public administration as much as it does adjudication) that to act in good faith and listen fairly to both sides is the duty lying upon everyone who decides anything."

13) Right to sufficient information

Bushell v Secretary of State for the Environment (1981)
Lord Diplock

"Fairness requires that the objector .... be given sufficient information about the reasons relied on by the Department as justifying the draft scheme to enable them to challenge the accuracy of any facts and the validity of any arguments upon which the departmental reasons are based"

14) Right to cross-examine

Osgood v Nelson (1872)
Baron Martin

There can be no doubt my Lords that the Courts of Law in this country, would take care that any proceeding in this country were conducted in a proper manner; that the person proposed who was to be removed should have every opportunity of cross-examining the witnesses brought forward against him, or otherwise opposing the case up against him; that he should have the power of calling witnesses to prove his own case; and he should have every possible opportunity which a person can have, according to the law and constitution of this country, of defending himself and of establishing that he is not liable to a motion"

>Bushell v Secretary of State for the Environment (1981)
>Lord Edmond-Davies

>"There is a massive body of accepted decisions establishing that natural justice requires that a party be given an opportunity of challenging by cross-examination witnesses called by another party on relevant issues."

15) Right to legitimate expectation

>Council of Civil Service Unions v Ministry of the Civil Service (1985) Lord Roskill

"The principle (of legitimate expectation) may (include) ………. an expectation of being allowed to undertake representations especially where the aggrieved party is seeking to persuade an authority to depart from a lawfully established policy adopted in connection with the exercise of a particular power because of some suggested exceptional reasons justifying such a departure."

>R v Secretary of State for The Home Department ex parte Ahmed (1999)
>Lord Justice Hobhouse

"The principle of legitimate expectation and English law is a principle of fairness in the decision making process................"

16) Duty not to adopt an unduly rigid policy

R v Secretary of State for the Environment ex p.Brent London Borough Council (1982)

> "(The Minister is) entitled to have well in mind his policy. To this extent the reference to keep an open mind does not mean an empty mind. This mind must be kept ajar"

> R v Hampshire County Council ex parte W (1994)
> Justice Sedley

"What is required by the law is that, without falling into arbitrariness, decision makers must remember that policies are means of securing a consistent approach to individual cases, each of which is likely to differ from others. Each case must be considered, therefore, in the light of the policy, but not so that the policy automatically determines the outcome".

R v Ministry for Agriculture Fisheries and Food ex p Hamble Fisheries(Off shore) Ltd (1995) Justice Sedley

"In describing the two conflicting imperatives of public law "the first is that while a policy may be adopted for the exercise of a discretion it must not be applied with rigidity which excludes consideration of possible departure on individual cases............., the second is that a discretionary public law power must not be exercised arbitrarily or with partiality as between individuals or classes potentially affected by it............ the line between individual consideration and inconsistency, slender enough in theory, can be imperceptible in practice"

17) Duty to reconsider where an important error of fact is made known

R v Newham London Borough Council ex parte Begum

(1996)

"the decision cried out for review when the error, on so important a matter, was drawn to the council's attention by the claimant's solicitors .... A failure to reconsider the decision in these circumstances would in my judgement have been unlawful."

18) Duty not to be irrational

Bromley and London Borough Council v Greater
London Council (1983)   Lord Diplock

"Decisions that, looked at objectively, are so devoid of any plausible justification that no reasonable body of persons could have reached".

Council of Civil Service Unions v Minister for the Civil
Service (1985) Lord Diplock

"By irrationality I mean what can now be succinctly referred to as Wednesbury unreasonableness .... it applies to a decision which is so outrageous in its defiance of logic or of accepted moral standards that no sensible person who had applied his mind to the question to be decided could have arrived at it."

19) Right for the procedural process not to affect an unfair conclusion

Mahon v Air New Zealand Ltd (1984) - referring to the
rule of natural justice,   Lord Diplock

"that the decision to make the finding must be based on some material which tends logically to show the existence of facts consistent with the finding and that the reasoning supportive of the finding, if it be disclosed, is not logically   self-contradictory".

R v Housing Benefit Review Board of London Borough of Sutton ex parte Keegan (1995)

> Conclusion "was arrived at in the teeth of the evidence and was accordingly Wednesbury unreasonable"

Conclusion

The Court of Star Chamber was established in 1487 by Henry VII and was developed by Cardinal Wolsey as an instrument of royal power. It evolved new and simple methods of effecting justice taken from Roman Law by which the Common Law rules of evidence were dispensed with. It was hated as a symbol of royal despotism and abolished in 1641 by the Long Parliament.

In Secretary of State for the Home Department v. AF (2009), Lord Phillips of Worth Matravers said:

The best way of producing a fair trial is to ensure that a party to it has the fullest information of both the allegations that are made against him and the evidence relied upon in support of those allegations. Where the evidence is documentary, he should have access to the documents. Where the evidence consists of oral testimony, then he should be entitled to cross-examine the witnesses who give that testimony, whose identities should be disclosed.

In Al Rawi and others v Security Service and others (2011) UKSC 34 at §12, Lord Dyson similarly made clear the fundamental nature of the principles involved:

trials are conducted on the basis of the principle of natural justice. There are a number of strands to this.

A party has a right to know the case against him and the evidence on which it is based. He is entitled to have the opportunity to respond to any such evidence and to any submissions made by the other side. The other side may not advance contentions or adduce evidence of which he is kept in ignorance.

Al Rawi (supra), Lord Kerr
To be truly valuable, evidence must be capable of withstanding challenge. I go further. Evidence which has been insulated from challenge may positively mislead. It is precisely because of this that the right to know the case that one's opponent makes and to have the opportunity to challenge it occupies such a central place in the concept of a fair trial. To deny that right is to deny that party's right to participate properly in the proceedings.

Thus the laws of England with regard to Natural Justice, based on Common Law apply to everyone at all times.

DEFAMATION

COUNCILS CANNOT SUE FOR DEFAMATION BUT INDIVIDUALS CAN

The House of Lords' decision in Derbyshire County Council v Times Newspapers (1993) AC 534 in which it was held that a local authority had no right at common law to sue for libel to protect its governing or administrative reputation, because allowing it such a right would stifle public opinion and be contrary to the public interest restriction on bringing defamation claims only applies to central and local government.

Mr Justice Eady noted that: "From time to time, it has been emphasised how important it is for the court to be wary, in cases where a corporate entity is suing for libel, to ensure that it is not being 'put up' or used as a protective shield when the real gravamen of the defamatory words is to reflect upon the reputation of an individual or individuals."

Notwithstanding that decision, the position for local authorities at common law remains governed by the Derbyshire decision. Whether that common law position - that local authorities may not sue for defamation - has changed in England has been the focus of recent discussion around the Localism Act 2011 ("the 2011 Act"). The 2011 Act gives local authorities "...power to do anything that individuals generally may do". The question of whether this allows scope for overturning the Derbyshire decision was raised following a report that Rutland Council intended to raise defamation claims against three of its own councillors using powers under section 1 of the 2011 Act.

The issue was addressed during a debate on the Defamation Bill currently going through Westminster in which Lord McNally attempted to reassure Parliament that the courts would uphold the Derbyshire principle. He affirmed that it would be "contrary to the public interest for organs of government to be able to sue in defamation, and that it would be an undesirable fetter on freedom of speech". This is, perhaps, not altogether unsurprising, as the general power that is referred to above is intended to enable local authorities to better discharge their functions in compliance with the statutory duty of best value. It was not intended as a means of holding local authorities free from criticism, justified or otherwise.

Qualified Privilege
The law surrounding defamation is intended to protect the reputation of individuals and has been broadly defined as relating to statements which 'tend to lower the plaintiff in the estimation of right-thinking members of society generally'. Defamation covers both libel and slander. The offence of slander can include defamatory speech and gestures, while libel requires publication of the defamation, which can include
television and radio broadcasts in addition to written material.
There are four main questions which must be asked in bringing a successful claim for defamation:
Is the statement defamatory?
Does the statement refer to the claimant?
Has the statement been published?
Are there any relevant defences?

Defences
At present the main defences to defamation are as follows:
Justification: that the statement can be proved to be true.
Honest comment: that the person who made the statement had the right to make the comment, meaning that it was an honest comment made in the sphere of public interest.
Privilege: that the statement was made on a 'privileged' occasion and so is not subject to defamation proceedings.

Qualified privilege is to be distinguished from absolute privilege. Absolute privilege is a complete defence to any accusation of defamation and covers situations including
trials and Parliamentary debates. Qualified privilege is a weaker variant, and applies only to statements made in accordance with a specified list of situations laid out in
statute or in accordance with the common law test laid out below. Qualified privilege is also lost if it can be shown that the statement was made with malice, i.e. that malice was the 'dominant and improper motive'. Establishing malice would normally require a demonstration either of recklessness or dishonesty on the part of the person making the statement.

Councillors as a group are not automatically protected either by absolute or qualified privilege. Instead they must usually rely on the relevant defence established at common law for qualified privilege, namely that the councillor has a legal, social, or moral duty to impart the information and the recipient, normally the public or fellow councillors/officers, has an interest in or duty to receive the information.

A key legal case covering qualified privilege in relation to councillors was Horrocks v Lowe (1975) in which Lord Denning found that:

**'It is of the first importance that the members of a local authority should be able to speak their minds freely on a matter of interest in the locality. So long as they honestly believe what they say to be true, they are not to be made liable for defamation. They may be prejudiced and unreasonable. They may not get their facts right. They may give much offence to others. But so long as they are honest, they go clear. No councillor should be hampered in his criticisms by fear of an action for slander. He is not to be forever looking over his shoulder to see if what he says is
defamatory. He must be allowed to give his point of view, even if it is hotly disputed by others. This is essential to free discussion.'**

However, it is important to note that the above will certainly not apply to all statements made by councillors. It is likely that qualified privilege would be found to apply to statements made in full council or committee meetings, and might also extend to some internal working groups. The privilege would be more difficult to extend to general interactions with the public or third parties outside meetings.

Members may also be interested to note that the Defamation Act 1996 applied qualified privilege, subject to affected parties being able to supply an explanation or correction where necessary, to the following situations:

A fair and accurate report of proceedings at any public meeting or sitting in the United Kingdom of a local authority or local authority committee, the executive of that authority or a committee of that executive.

A fair and accurate record of any decision made by any member of the executive where that record is required to be made and available for public inspection by virtue of section 22 of the Local Government Act 2000 or of any provision in regulations made under that section.

In the UK, unlike some other common law jurisdictions, the media has no special status for qualified privilege, and, while their special role is recognised to an extent, must rely on the same defences as councillors or members of the public in
establishing qualified privilege.

THE LAW ON QUALIFIED PRIVILEDGE
(Easily explained)

Councillor Robert Horrocks (Conservative) won his case against Councillor Peter Lowe (Labour) before Judge Stirling (no jury). But Peter Lowe appealed to the Court of appeal and won his appeal overturning the lower court decision.   Then Robert Horrocks appealed to the House of Lords to overturn the Court of Appeal judgement but failed. The House of Lords upheld the decision of the Court of appeal.   The case is about "Qualified Privilege" and

"Express Malice".

(1975) 135 A.C. (HOUSE OF LORDS)

HORROCKS-APPELLANT
AND
LOWE-RESPONDENT
1973 Nov. 6, 7, 8; 1974 Jan. 30

Lord Wilberforce, Lord Hodson, Viscount Dilhorne, Lord Diplock and Lord Kilbrandon

Libel and Slander - Defamation - Privilege - Qualified - Council meeting - Defamatory words spoken by one councillor of another - Plea of express malice destroying qualified privilege - Finding that words spoken in honest belief of their truth but with gross, unreasoning prejudice - Whether constituting evidence of malice

In 1961 a corporation bought a piece of land from a company of which the plaintiff was chairman and majority shareholder. It was subject to a covenant that it would not be built on. The company sold adjoining plots and plots opposite the corporation's site to purchasers on that understanding. In 1968, when the plaintiff was a councillor of the majority party on the town council, the corporation granted a lease of the land to a political party club for the purpose of building a club house. Not until the building was nearing completion was it discovered that the covenant prohibited the development of the land. The plaintiff's company had the benefit of the covenant and correspondence passed between the council officers and the company's solicitors, but the company was reluctant to release the covenant, in the interests of the surrounding purchasers. The defendant, an alderman in the minority party, raised the matter in council, and in the course of a speech at an open council meeting he uttered words defamatory of the plaintiff. The plaintiff brought an action for slander against the defendant who by his defence claimed justification and fair comment on a privileged occasion. By his reply the plaintiff pleaded that the defendant had been actuated by express malice. Stirling J. held that the occasion had been privileged. He found that the defendant had honestly believed that what he said was true, but that he had shown such "gross and unreasoning prejudice" as to constitute malice in law sufficient to destroy the privilege. He awarded the plaintiff damages. **On appeal by the defendant, the Court of Appeal held, allowing the appeal, that as the judge had found that the defendant had honestly believed that what he said was true the qualified privilege attaching to the occasion could only be destroyed if the plaintiff proved that the defendant had been actuated by express malice in its popular meaning of spite or ill will, and that as such express malice had not been found the finding of malice could not stand with the finding of honest belief, so that the privilege of the occasion had protected the defendant.**

On appeal by the plaintiff:-

Held, dismissing the appeal, that since the defendant had not misused the privileged occasion by using it for some purpose other than that for which the privilege was accorded to it in the public interest his positive belief in the truth of what he said entitled him to succeed in his defence of qualified privilege (post, pp. 142G-H, 145H - 146B, D-H, 149E-F, 150B-C,E-F, 151F-G, 152A-B, D-G, 153F-G).

Clark v. Molyneux (1877) 3 Q.B.D. 237, C.A. and dicta of Lord Dunedin in Adam v. Ward (1917) A.C. 309, 326-327, 330, H.L.(E.) applied.
Royal Aquarium and Summer and Winter Garden Society Ltd. v. Parkinson (1892) 1 Q.B. 431, C.A. and Watt v. Longsdon (1930) 1 K.B. 130, C.A. considered.
Decision of the Court of Appeal (1972) 1 W.L.R. 1625; (1972) 3 All E.R. 1098 affirmed.
The following cases are referred to in their Lordships' opinions:

Adam v. Ward (1917) A.C. 309, H.L.(E.).

Clark v. Molyneux (1877) 3 Q.B.D. 237; 47 L.J.Q.B. 230, C.A.

Laughton v. Bishop of Sodor and Man (1872) L.R. 4 P.C. 495, P.C.

Royal Aquarium and Summer and Winter Garden Society Ltd. v. Parkinson (1892) 1 Q.B. 431, C.A.

Smith v. Thomas (1835) 2 Bing.N.C. 372.

Watt v. Longsdon (1930) 1 K.B. 130, C.A.

The following additional cases were cited in argument:

Broadway Approvals Ltd. v. Odhams Press Ltd. (No. 2) (1965) 1 W.L.R. 805; (1965) 2 All E.R. 523, C.A.

Brown v. Hawkes (1891) 2 Q.B. 718, C.A.

Coughlan v. Jones and Jones (1915) 35 N.Z.L.R. 41.

Dawkins v. Lord Paulet (1869) L.R. 5 Q.B. 94.

Derry v. Peek (1889) 14 App.Cas. 337, H.L.(E.).

Dickson v. Earl of Wilton (1859) 1 F. & F. 419.

Hayford v. Forrester-Paton, 1927 S.C. 740.

Merivale v. Carson (1887) 20 Q.B.D. 275, C.A.

Pitt v. Donovan (1813) 1 M. & S. 639.

Pratt v. British Medical Association (1919) 1 K.B. 244.

Silkin v. Beaverbrook Newspapers Ltd. (1958) 1 W.L.R. 743; (1958) 2 All E.R. 516.

Simpson v. Robinson (1848) 18 L.J.Q.B. 73.

Slim v. Daily Telegraph Ltd. (1968) 2 Q.B. 157; (1968) 2 W.L.R. 599; (1968) 1 All E.R. 497, C.A.

Spill v. Maule (1869) L.R. 4 Exch. 232.

Turner (orse. Robertson) v. Metro-Goldwyn-Mayer Pictures Ltd. (1950) 1 All E.R. 449, H.L.(E.).

Webb v. Bloch (1928) 41 C.L.R. 331.

Winstanley v. Bampton (1943) K.B. 319; (1943) 1 All E.R. 661.

APPEAL from the Court of Appeal (Lord Denning M.R., Edmund Davies and Stephenson L.JJ.) (1972) 1 W.L.R. 1625.

This was an appeal by the plaintiff, Robert Horrocks, by leave of the House granted on December 19, 1972, from a decision of the Court of Appeal on October 6, 1973, reversing a decision of Stirling J. sitting without a jury at Manchester by which he awarded the plaintiff £400 damages for slander against the defendant, Peter Lowe.

The plaintiff, at all material times a councillor of Bolton Town Council, by his statement of claim alleged that the words of a speech delivered by the defendant at a meeting of the council on November 5, 1969, and a report of the council meeting published on November 6, 1969, in the "Bolton Evening News" were calculated to disparage him in his office and business. By his defence the defendant, inter alia, claimed that the words were spoken to persons having a common interest and in pursuance of a duty without malice in the honest belief that they were true, and on an occasion of qualified privilege. By his reply the plaintiff claimed that in publishing the words complained of the defendant was actuated by express malice.

Stirling J. found that the words used were defamatory and could not be justified and while he was prepared to accept "that he (the defendant) believed and still believes that everything he said was true and justifiable" he found that as a whole the speech was such an unfair and tendentious account of the plaintiff's conduct in relation to the relevant land that it established "gross and unreasoning prejudice," and he awarded the plaintiff £400 in respect of the slander and costs. On the defendant's appeal, the Court of Appeal (1972) 1 W.L.R. 1625 held that the defendant's belief that everything he said was true entitled him to succeed on his defence of privilege.

The plaintiff appealed.

The facts are stated in the opinion of Lord Diplock.

Colin Duncan Q.C. and John E. Previtz for the plaintiff. This appeal raises a short question of law, which was wrongly decided by the Court of Appeal, namely, in any action for libel or slander in which defamatory words have been published on an occasion of qualified privilege, and it is alleged that the defendant was actuated by express malice, and evidence of such malice is adduced at the trial and malice is found established, either by a jury or by a judge, is it in law impossible to find for the plaintiff if it is accepted that the defendant believed what he published at the time of its publication, albeit such belief is found to have been induced by gross, unreasoning prejudice?

"Honest belief" is on the face of it a most misleading expression. Belief either exists or does not exist. "Honest belief" presupposes the possibility of a dishonest belief, which is nonsense. Cotton L.J. in Clark v. Molyneux (1877) 47 L.J.Q.B. 230, 233 described the expression as an inaccurate one. "Honest belief" is perhaps meant to mean a belief arrived at after examination of the relevant factors, though by no means a reasonable conclusion drawn from them.

What is meant by "express malice" in law? Malice is, of course, a state of mind and not conduct, as Lord Esher M.R. said in Royal Aquarium and Summer and Winter Garden Society Ltd. v. Parkinson (1892) 1 Q.B. 431, 444. A short definition of malice is that it is a state of mind which prompts the defendant to use the privileged occasion for any purpose other than that for which the privilege exists. There are five characteristic sets of circumstances in which malice may be evidenced. (First, however, see Salmond on Torts, 16th ed. (1973), para. 162, pp. 176-177, for an accurate definition of malice in law.) In no particular order, the five sets of circumstances are: 1. The violence of the language used which will not be a feature of the plaintiff's argument here. This is not to be weighed too nicely, but is a factor to be taken into account. 2. Where the defendant publishes what he knows to be untrue. This is the strongest pointer, but it is not necessarily conclusive; for example, an army officer passes on a report which he knows to be untrue but which it is his duty to pass on. This category does not apply in the present case either: there was a finding by Stirling J.

that the defendant believed what he published to be true.

(LORD DIPLOCK. Are these circumstances from which malice can be inferred or from which it must be inferred?)

Generally, they are circumstances from which it can be inferred. In one of them, however, it must be. So far as 1 is concerned, for example, it can, and in general should, be inferred. So far as 2 is concerned, only in exceptional circumstances would it not be. As a counterpart to 2, the fact that a defendant publishes what he knows to be true does not mean that he cannot be actuated by express malice. The Court of Appeal in the present case have held that the defendant did not publish what he knew to be true.

3. Where the defendant believes what he says to be true, but is using the occasion not for the purpose for which the privilege exists but for an independent and improper purpose. This applies directly to this case. "Improper" is not used in any moral sense. 4. Here, one starts with the premises that the defendant may believe what he publishes to be true and may not be inspired by any improper motive, so that 2 and 3 are excluded. As a result of gross, unreasoning prejudice, however, the defendant had allowed his mind to become obsessed and by the time of publication of the defamatory matter has closed his mind. He believes in the truth of his charges because he wants to believe them. The judge so found in this case. 5. Spite or ill will - one of the commonest grounds. This was expressly found to be excluded in this case.

The defendant here in fact used the occasion for an improper purpose, he had an ulterior motive for publishing what he did and he had allowed his mind to get into a state in which it was actuated by gross, unreasoning prejudice.

A most important feature in considering malice is that the judge or jury at first instance has a unique opportunity of seeing the witnesses. On May 5, 1971, here, the trial began at Manchester. It lasted five days.

At the end of the first day the jury were dispensed with; the judge therefore became the sole judge of fact. That is a factor of great importance.

The evidence discloses that the defendant failed to consider the facts, and, therefore, that he was reckless. A mere unreasonable assessment of the facts is in itself incapable of establishing malice unless it is so far from the truth that it shows gross, unreasoning prejudice. A distinction is to be drawn between "unreasonable" and "unreasoning." It is clear from the evidence in this case that the defendant regarded this meeting as an opportunity for attacking the plaintiff, not, for example, for getting any facts out of him.

The principle emerges from Clark v. Molyneux, 3 Q.B.D. 237 (see also 47 L.J.Q.B. 230, 233), and more from Winstanley v. Bampton (1943) K.B. 319, that honest belief does not necessarily mean that a defendant is not guilty of malice. Clark v. Molyneux also shows (see also 47 L.J.Q.B. 230, 233) that abuse of the occasion is not a state of mind; it is a fact which follows a state of mind. (The same applies to fair comment.) (Reference was made to Smith v. Thomas (1835) 2 Bing.N.C. 372, 382; Dickson v. Earl of Wilton (1859) 1 F. & F. 419; Simpson v. Robinson (1848) 18 L.J.Q.B. 73; Broadway Approvals Ltd. v. Odhams Press Ltd. (No. 2) (1965) 1 W.L.R. 805; Merivale v. Carson (1887) 20 Q.B.D. 275, per Lord Esher M.R., at p. 281; Brown v. Hawkes (1891) 2 Q.B. 718; Royal Aquarium and Summer and Winter Garden Society Ltd. v. Parkinson (1892) 1 Q.B. 431; Coughlan v. Jones and Jones (1915) 35 N.Z.L.R. 41, 44; Pratt v. British Medical Association (1919) 1 K.B. 244, 276; Webb v. Bloch (1928) 41 C.L.R. 331 and Watt v. Longsdon (1930) 1 K.B. 130.) Winstanley v. Bampton (1943) K.B. 319 shows that honest belief, or belief, does not destroy other evidence of malice. Viscount Caldecote C.J., at p. 322; (1943) 1 All E.R. 661, 663 refers to Watt v. Longsdon (1930) 1 K.B. 130 as authority, not merely to the observations of Greer L.J. in that case.

It is part of the plaintiff's case that the defendant failed to make any reference to the embarrassments which he knew the plaintiff had to his "dilemma": compare Broadway Approvals Ltd. v. Odhams Press Ltd. (No. 2) (1965) 1 W.L.R. 805, per Sellers L.J., at p. 814, per Davies L.J., at p. 824.

Previtz following. Not only was it part of the plaintiff's case at the trial that the defendant had misused the occasion, but it was also his submission to the Court of Appeal.

The purpose of the meeting was the removal of the plaintiff. It was not an appropriate occasion for asking for the removal of a man from the committee. That was not the subject matter of the meeting, which was concerned with the council's liability to pay compensation. By raising the matter in the way the defendant did the effect was that the plaintiff had to be excluded from the meeting. The plaintiff does not say that seeking to get him off the committee was an improper motive, but using that occasion for that end was.

Lord Denning M.R. in the instant case elevated qualified privilege to a situation of absolute privilege.

A summary of the information which was available to the defendant as at November 5, 1969, shows that the defendant had a closed mind.

(LORD WILBERFORCE. The House wishes the defendant to address it on the subject of gross, unreasoning prejudice and how it fits in with honest belief. He need not address it on the question of the appropriateness of the occasion.)

Michael Kempster Q.C. and Patrick Milmo for the defendant. The plaintiff served a reply setting out the particulars of express malice on which he proposed to rely as required by R.S.C., Ord. 82, r. 3 (3).

Further particulars were served in the course of the trial. There was no mention in either set of particulars and no allegation, of the defendant's simple intention of securing the exclusion of the plaintiff from the relevant committee, and no other matters were set out from which "recklessness" could properly be inferred. It appears from the judgment of Stirling J., however, that in fact that motive was employed in argument by leading counsel not as a separate motive from which malice was to be inferred but as a precipitating matter giving rise to the defendant's "closed mind," prejudice, and in turn to recklessness. It was argued that the defendant had that motive, that that led to his mind being closed and unreasonable and that that led to recklessness. This is consistent with the grounds in the plaintiff's further particulars of his reply from which malice was to be inferred. Stirling J. found (1) that the words spoken were defamatory; (2) that they were spoken on an occasion of qualified privilege; (3) that the defendant was labouring under unreasoning prejudice and had a closed mind at the time when the words complained of were spoken. He might have meant that that was evidence either of malice or of a closed mind. Then, however, one comes to the passage in his judgment from which it is clear that he regarded those matters as no more than factors on which one could properly rely in finding that the defendant had had a closed mind. Stirling J. made no finding of recklessness. Prejudice in itself is not an indication from which malice is to be inferred. Stirling J. found that the nature of the defendant's speech - by reason of its being unfair and tendentious - established gross and unreasoning prejudice.

A man cannot be reckless if he honestly and genuinely believes. The finding of Stirling J. that the defendant's unreasoning prejudice was in itself an indication from which malice was to be inferred, at the same time as he found honest belief, was an error which the Court of Appeal properly pointed out. Stirling J. found that the defendant believed that everything which he did was true and justifiable. He did not find recklessness, abuse of the occasion of privilege, that the defendant was moved by hatred for or dislike

of or desire to calumniate or injure the plaintiff or anyone else (cf. Watt v. Longsdon (1930) 1 K.B. 130) or that he acted otherwise than from a sense of duty.

In those circumstances, where honest belief has been found and the defendant has been found not to have been actuated by any improper motive, there can properly be a finding not just of belief but of honest belief.

If every word and adjective must be given effect to, then when the Court of Appeal use the words "honest belief" - not specifically used by Stirling J. but referred to by him in a reference to Royal Aquarium and Summer and Winter Garden Society Ltd. v. Parkinson (1892) 1 Q.B. 431 - they are in effect saying that not only was the defendant's belief genuine but also he was acting bona fide, within the ambit of privilege (see Spencer Bower on Actionable Defamation, 2nd ed. (1923), p. 398). The effect of Stirling J.'s findings, and of what he did not find, was that there was genuine belief and no improper motive. That could be described as "honest belief." **The Court of Appeal held, correctly, that recklessness and belief could not coexist: see per Lord Denning M.R. (1972) 1 W.L.R. 1625, 1631.**

To find "gross and unreasoning prejudice" of a defendant does not mean that he is reckless. He does apply his mind to the matter, and then forms a prejudice. If he refuses to look at something, that might come near to recklessness, but if belief exists then a man is entitled to enjoy the privilege. That is the effect of the line of authorities. The test is always a subjective one, never objective. **The judge or jury must always look into the mind of the defendant, and not apply the standard of the reasonable man. They must not look at whether the defendant was reasoning or unreasoning.**

The first of this line of authorities was Pitt v. Donovan (1813) 1 M. & S. 639. (Reference was made to Spill v. Maule (1869) L.R. 4 Exch. 232; Clark v. Molyneux, 3 Q.B.D. 237; Adam v. Ward (1917) A.C.

309; Hayford v. Forrester-Paton, 1927 S.C. 740; Turner (orse. Robertson) v. Metro-Goldwyn-Mayer Pictures Ltd. (1950) 1 All E.R. 449; Slim v. Daily Telegraph Ltd. (1968) 2 Q.B. 157 and Silkin v. Beaverbrook Newspapers Ltd. (1958) 1 W.L.R. 743.)

In summary, Stirling J.'s findings amount to findings both of genuine belief and of absence of any improper motive. They amount to findings of honest belief in the sense suggested by Spencer Bower on Actionable Defamation, 2nd ed., p. 398. Accordingly, the Court of Appeal was right in allowing the appeal and saying that honest belief disposed of recklessness, and that prejudice on its own was not a basis on which malice could be found. The Court of Appeal were right again because when, in a situation of privilege, one examines the mind of the speaker, one does not test his mind by reference to an objective standard but the object is (1) to see whether belief is established: Stirling J. so found here, and it is inconsistent with recklessness. Without recklessness, prejudice does not defeat the privilege. (2) Malice could still be established by abuse of the occasion. It is conceded that the authorities show that in certain cases a man may have a belief in the truth of what he says and yet be fixed with malice, because to maintain a situation of privilege he must not only believe, or honestly believe, but must make his statement for the purpose for which the privilege is allowed him.

The most economical statement of the position where privilege is admitted and malice alleged is by Cockburn C.J. in Dawkins v. Lord Paulet (1869) L.R. 5 Q.B. 94, 102. See also the malicious prosecution case of Brown v. Hawkes (1891) 2 Q.B. 718; a passage in the judgment of Cave J. which was there upheld, at p. 722, is of assistance. (Reference was made to Derry v. Peek (1889) 14 App.Cas. 337, 376.) Some of what Greer L.J. says in Watt v. Longsdon (1930) 1 K.B. 130, 154 is obiter and wrong. **Watt v. Longsdon shows that malice could still be found in spite of a sense of duty if the writer is actuated by a sense of spite or ill will in the sense of the traditional meaning of malice.** In Royal Aquarium and

Summer and Winter Garden Society Ltd. v. Parkinson (1892) 1 Q.B.

431 Lord Esher M.R. says, at p. 436, that prejudice may be the cause of recklessness but that one has to look for recklessness.

Duncan Q.C. in reply. On Royal Aquarium and Summer and Winter Garden Society Ltd. v. Parkinson (1892) 1 Q.B. 431, see the reference to that case by McCardie J. in Pratt v. British Medical Association (1919) 1 K.B. 244, 276. There are no findings on fair comment. There is a finding that the statements of fact were untrue, so the matters complained of cannot be fair comment. Fair comment is an expression of opinion and belief or honest belief in the truth of the statement does not arise. It is quite different from a statement of fact. Whether the test of recklessness is objective or subjective is a double test. **One has to ask whether a reasonable person could possibly have made the statement, and what was the motive of the person who did make it.**

The statement of claim is accepted as being the accurate version of what the defendant said. As to the defendant's attempt on this appeal to list the material which was in the defendant's mind when he said that the plaintiff had misled the committee, there is no evidence to support that list other than what the defendant himself said at the trial.

Stirling J. found that the defendant was actuated by express malice. He found that he was actuated by unreasoning prejudice and had a closed mind. He found that he misused the occasion. He found that he was reckless. The "reckless" finding should be related to the paragraph before: plaintiff's leading counsel at the trial was well founded in what he said.

The question which the plaintiff has to face is this: can one have an honest belief at the same time as being reckless? Reckless means paying insufficient regard to factors as a result of prejudice leading to a position in which one has a closed mind and does not approach the problem with a reasoning mind, as sharply distinguished from a reasonable mind. A person may be unreasonable although he has taken great pains to discover the answer. In the present case, however, as Stirling J. found, the defendant was actuated by prejudice into having a closed mind. That is sufficient to establish recklessness.

If honest belief is to have any meaning at all it must be accepted that it is inconsistent with a reckless state of mind. One must, however, distinguish between honest belief and belief induced by recklessness, which is what Stirling J. found. He does not say "honest belief"; that is significant.

Their Lordships took time for consideration.

January 30. LORD WILBERFORCE. My Lords, I have had the advantage of reading in advance the opinion of my noble and learned friend, Lord Diplock, with which I concur.

I would dismiss the appeal.

LORD HODSON. My Lords, for the reasons given by my noble and learned friend, Lord Diplock, I, too, would dismiss the appeal.

VISCOUNT DILHORNE. My Lords, the respondent was at all material times an alderman of the Bolton Town Council, a member of a number of its committees and of the Labour party, which was then in a minority on the council. The appellant was also a member of the council. He was a member of its Management and Finance Committee and a Conservative. The Conservatives then held a majority on the council. The appellant was also chairman and the majority shareholder in a holding company called Land Development and Building Ltd. Among the activities of its subsidiary companies were the sale, purchase and development of land.

The company sold to the corporation some land subject to a

restrictive covenant preventing building thereon. Houses were built on adjoining land and let by a company in which the appellant was concerned on the basis that the land subject to the restrictive covenant would not be built on so that the frontagers would not have the view from their houses obstructed.

Unfortunately the Bolton Corporation, when letting some of the land in Bishops Road to the Great Lever Conservative Club for the club to build premises thereon, overlooked the existence of the covenant. When its existence was brought to their knowledge efforts were made without success to secure the release of the land from the covenant, one difficulty being the assurances given to the frontagers that the land would not be built on. As no release was obtained the Management and Finance Committee ultimately decided that alternative accommodation should be found for the club and compensation paid to them. As a great deal of the building had been done the compensation was considerable.

At the meeting of the Management and Finance Committee at which this was decided and at which the appellant, on account of his interest in the matter, was not present, the respondent expressed the view that the appellant should not be a member of that committee because of the frequency with which his professional interests were likely to arise in matters of concern to the committee. He gave notice of his intention to raise the matter at a meeting of the council. With a Conservative majority on the council he thought his chances of getting his view accepted were slight, but he thought that the Bishops Road fiasco, as it was called, gave him the opportunity he wanted. Prior to November 5, 1969, the Labour caucus met and it was decided that the appellant should be attacked on account of his failure to secure the release of the restrictive covenant and that an effort should be made to secure his removal from the Management and Finance Committee. It was agreed that the respondent should make the attack.

At the meeting of the council on November 5, 1969, he did so. In the course of his speech, which consisted mainly of a narration of events in relation to the building on the restricted land and to the efforts made to secure the release of the covenant, he made some offensive personal observations about the appellant who, again on account of his interest in the matter, was not present, saying:

"For two months he has been like Achilles sulking in his tent while we waited for news. I don't know how to describe his attitude whether it was brinkmanship, megalomania or childish petulance" and

"I suggest that he has misled the committee, the leader of his party and his political and club colleagues some of whom are his business associates."

The appellant issued a writ claiming inter alia damages for slander in respect of this speech.

Stirling J., who tried the case, held that the passages in the speech which I have quoted were defamatory. He held that there had been nothing in the appellant's conduct which could justifiably be the object of any criticism whatever. He saw no evidence that the appellant was capricious, unduly dilatory, or inconsistent or in any way underhand or dishonourable. **He ruled that the speech was made on an occasion of qualified privilege, so whether the appellant succeeded in his action depended on whether or not he could establish that the respondent was actuated by malice.**

Stirling J. came to the conclusion that the respondent was so anxious to have the appellant removed from the Management and Finance Committee that he did not consider fairly and objectively whether the evidence he had in his possession justified his conclusions or comments. Stirling J. regarded his speech as a whole as such an unfair and tendentious assessment of the appellant's conduct that it established gross and unreasoning prejudice on the respondent's part, but he accepted that the respondent believed, and at the trial believed, that everything he had said was true and justifiable.

Founding apparently on a passage in Gatley on Libel and Slander, 6th ed. (1967), para. 770, which says:
"If a man, through anger, or gross and unreasoning prejudice, has allowed his mind to get into such a state - to become so obsessed - as to cast reckless aspersions on other people which but for such state of mind he could not have honestly believed to be true, the jury may properly find that he has abused the occasion, and in that sense has acted maliciously."

and a passage from the judgment of Lord Esher M.R. in Royal Aquarium and Summer and Winter Garden Society Ltd. v. Parkinson (1892) 1 Q.B. 431, he held that there was malice on the part of the respondent due to his unreasoning prejudice even though he believed what he said. Stirling J. therefore gave judgment for the appellant.

I must confess to feeling considerable doubt whether the finding that there was gross and unreasoning prejudice on the part of the respondent was justified. The respondent was entitled to hold the view that the appellant should not, on account of his business interests, be a member of the Management and Finance Committee. He was clearly not abusing the privileged occasion in expressing that view. In Adam v. Ward (1917) A.C. 309, Lord Dunedin said, at p. 330: "... when considering whether the actual expression used can be held as evidence of express malice no nice scales should be used." Lord Dunedin went on to cite the following passage from the judgment of the Privy Council in Laughton v. Bishop of Sodor and Man (1872) L.R. 4 P.C. 495, 508:

"To submit the language of privileged communications to a strict scrutiny, and to hold all excess beyond the absolute exigency of the occasion to be evidence of malice would in effect greatly limit, if not altogether defeat, that protection which the law throws

over privileged communications."

And in Clark v. Molyneux (1877) 3 Q.B.D. 237, Cotton L.J. observed, at p. 249:

"In order to show that the defendant was acting with malice, it is not enough to show a want of reasoning power or stupidity, for those things of themselves do not constitute malice: a man may be wanting in reasoning power, or he may be very stupid, still he may be acting bona fide, honestly intending to discharge a duty."

These observations which I have cited were directed to the issue whether there was or was not express malice, but I think that in considering whether or not there was gross and unreasoning prejudice on the part of the respondent no nice scales should be used and that the fact that he made observations and comments which others would not have thought it justified or right to make does not, to my mind, exclude the possibility that they were made, not on account of prejudice, but by reason of his failure to appreciate the inadequacy of the grounds on which he based his comments.

However this may be, the question now to be decided is whether the finding of malice, based on Stirling J.'s conclusion that there was gross and unreasoning prejudice, can stand in view of his finding that the respondent believed what he said.

If a man abuses a privileged occasion by making defamatory statements which he knows to be false, express malice may easily be inferred. If, on such an occasion, he makes statements recklessly, not caring whether they be true or false, again malice may be inferred. Such recklessness may be induced by anger, as Lord Esher M.R. pointed out in Royal Aquarium and Summer and Winter Garden Society Ltd. v. Parkinson (1892) 1 Q.B. 431, 444. Lord Esher M.R. went on to say that gross and unreasoning prejudice

"... not only with regard to particular people, but with regard to a subject matter in question, would have the same effect. If a person charged with the duty of dealing with other people's rights and interests has allowed his mind to fall into such a state of unreasoning prejudice in regard to the subject matter that he was reckless whether what he stated was true or false, there would be evidence upon which a jury might say that he abused the occasion."

Lord Esher M.R. was pointing out that there was a state of mind, short of deliberate falsehood, which may lead to the conclusion that there was an abuse of the privileged occasion. He was not dealing with the case where a man honestly believes the truth of his statements.

Can a man who believes what he says on a privileged occasion to be true and which if true would not be an abuse of the occasion be held to have made his statements "recklessly whether they are true or false"? Gross and unreasoning prejudice may have led him to have uttered them recklessly whether they were true or false, but if he believes the truth of what he said, can he at the same time be said to be reckless of the truth or falsity of his statements? May be that others with more judgment and more wisdom would not have formed the same belief, but if, in fact, he believes what he says, he cannot at the same time, in my opinion, be reckless whether it is true or false. Such recklessness falls short of deliberate falsehood. But such recklessness, not minding or caring whether it be true or false, whether it arise from anger or unreasoning prejudice, or from some other cause, is not consistent with belief in the truth of the statement.

In Watt v. Longsdon (1930) 1 K.B. 130, Greer L.J. said, at p. 154:

"A man may believe in the truth of a defamatory statement, and yet when he publishes it be reckless whether his belief be well founded or not. His motive for publishing a libel on a privileged occasion may be an improper one, even though he believes the statement to be true."

If the statements were believed to be true, that negatives malice based on the contentions that the defendant did not believe them to be true and made them recklessly not caring whether they were true or false. But malice may be established in other ways than showing that the defendant did not believe in the truth of what he said (Smith v. Thomas (1835) 2 Bing.N.C. 372, 382, per Tindal C.J.).

While it is true that a man may believe in the truth of what he says and yet be reckless whether his belief is well founded or not, recklessness whether the belief is well founded, while relevant to the question whether the defendant believed what he said, is not, if the defendant in fact believed, evidence of malice. If it were, then the man who honestly and out of a sense of duty made observations based on information found to be inaccurate or incorrect would have his freedom of speech on a privileged occasion unduly restricted. In this connection the observations of Cotton L.J. in Clark v. Molyneux, 3 Q.B.D. 237, 249 which I have cited are relevant.

In my opinion, the Court of Appeal were right to allow the respondent's appeal. In the course of delivering their judgments some observations were made by their Lordships which might, if taken out of their context, be interpreted as laying down general principles. In this case the only question was whether malice could be inferred from the lack of foundation for the statements made and their tendentious quality, which led Stirling J. to hold that there was gross and unreasoning prejudice and malice despite his finding that the respondent believed what he said. To that, the belief of the respondent was, in my opinion, a complete answer. I do not believe Lord Denning M.R.'s observation ((1972) 1 W.L.R. 1625, 1630) that members of a local authority, so long as they believe what they say to be true, are not liable for defamation, and when he said: "... so long as they are honest, they go clear," was meant to apply generally and not just to the facts of this case. For a man who honestly believes what he says may yet be actuated by malice and such malice may be established by other evidence than the inference to be drawn from the falsity of the statement. It is that inference which is negatived by belief. For these reasons, in my opinion, this appeal should be dismissed.

LORD DIPLOCK. My Lords, at a meeting of the Bolton Borough Council in November 1969 the respondent, Alderman Lowe, made a speech criticising the conduct of the appellant, Councillor Horrocks, both as a member of the Management and Finance Committee of the council and as chairman of a company, Land Development and Building Ltd. The speech concluded with a request that Mr. Horrocks should be removed from that committee. The words used were defamatory of Mr. Horrocks. He brought an action for slander against Mr. Lowe. At the trial at Manchester Assizes before Stirling J., sitting without a jury, Mr. Lowe's counsel did not seek to justify the expressions used. He relied on the defence of qualified privilege. The judge held, as has never been disputed, that the words were spoken on a privileged occasion; but he also held that malice on the part of Mr. Lowe had been established and gave judgment for the plaintiff for £400 damages. It is only fair to Mr. Horrocks to say that the judge found that the criticism of his conduct was quite unjustified. The only reason why the award of damages was low was because he made it clear through his counsel that what he sought was not substantial damages, but to reinstate his reputation.

Stirling J. found expressly that Mr. Lowe "believed and still believes that everything he said was true and justifiable, ..." He also found, however, that owing to Mr. Lowe's anxiety to have Mr. Horrocks removed from the Management and Finance Committee his state of mind was one of "gross and unreasoning prejudice" - a phrase borrowed from the judgment of Lord Esher M.R. in Royal Aquarium and Summer and Winter Garden Society Ltd. v. Parkinson (1892) 1 Q.B. 431, 444. That case he regarded as "authority for the proposition that such an attitude of mind, if proved, is evidence from which a jury could properly infer malice even if honest belief in the words used exists."

Paragraph 770 of the current (6th) edition of Gatley on Libel and Slander, the only book to which he was referred in Manchester, appears to support this view.

It will become necessary to examine in more detail some of the judge's other findings as to Mr. Lowe's conduct and attitude of mind; but the finding that the defendant believed that everything he said was true and justifiable lies at the root of this appeal. It was the only part of Stirling J.'s judgment that was dealt with in the judgments of the Court of Appeal on Mr. Lowe's appeal. He conducted his own case in person there, and succeeded upon the ground that his belief that everything he said was true made it impossible as a matter of law to find that he was actuated by malice.

The judgments of Lord Denning M.R. and Edmund Davies L.J. have been criticised in your Lordships' House as being based upon too broad a proposition of law. It is true that there are passages in these extempore judgments which might be read as suggesting that where on a privileged occasion a defendant publishes defamatory statements which he believes to be true he can only lose the protection of the privilege on proof that he was actuated by personal spite against the person defamed. But the Court of Appeal were not embarking on a general exposition of the law of privilege in actions for defamation. Their attention was concentrated upon the particular facts of the instant case as they had been found in the judgment of Stirling J. Upon those facts the Court of Appeal's decision that Mr. Lowe's belief that everything he said was true entitled him to succeed on his defence of privilege was in my view correct.

The facts are set out in detail in the unreported judgment of Stirling

J. They are summarised with his customary felicity in the reported judgment of Lord Denning M.R. in (1972) 1 W.L.R. 1625. Those which are essential to dispose of the question of law now before your Lordships' House can be stated even more briefly.

The business of the Bolton Borough Council was conducted by its members on party political lines. Mr. Horrocks was a member of the Conservative caucus which at the relevant time was in a majority. Mr. Lowe was a member of the Labour caucus. Both were members of the important Management and Finance Committee of the council. Mr. Horrocks was also chairman and majority shareholder in Land Development and Building Ltd., a property company engaged in dealing in and developing property within the borough. In 1961 this company had sold to the Bolton Corporation some land in Bishops Road subject to a restrictive covenant against building on it. Later the company sold building plots on some of the remainder of the land assuring the purchasers of these plots that nothing would be built on the land that had been conveyed to the corporation. Unfortunately, this restrictive covenant was overlooked by the officials of the corporation when a 99-year lease of part of the land subject to it was later granted to the Conservative Club for the erection of a club house. Building work had proceeded nearly to roof height when, in August 1969, the company's solicitors drew the attention of the corporation and the club to the restrictive covenant and demanded that the building be removed.

The matter was dealt with at meetings of the Management and Finance Committee of which the chairman was a Conservative, Alderman Telford. Mr. Lowe was present, but Mr. Horrocks, because of his personal interest, absented himself when the matter was discussed. No solution to the difficulty could be found and ultimately the corporation accepted the liability to find another site for the Conservative Club and to pay them very substantial compensation for their wasted expenditure. A statement to this effect was to be made at the meeting of the borough council of

November 5, 1969, by Alderman Telford.

Mr. Lowe and other members of the Labour caucus took the view that because of his personal interest in the development of land in Bolton Mr. Horrocks ought not to be a member of the Management and Finance Committee. He had expressed this view at the meeting of that committee on October 27, 1969, but was powerless to obtain acceptance of it by the committee because of the Conservative majority on the committee and in the council itself. He gave notice that he intended to raise the matter again at the council meeting on November 5 on the occasion of the statement by Alderman Telford about the Bishops Road site. This he did, and what he said at that meeting of the council is the slander in respect of which this action has been brought. It consisted in large part of a recital of what he understood to be the facts about the Bishops Road affair. It was hard hitting criticism of Mr. Horrocks's conduct. The sting of it was in the words quoted by Stirling J.:

"I don't know how to describe his attitude whether it was brinkmanship, megalomania or childish petulance ... I suggest that he has misled the committee, the leader of his party and his political and club colleagues some of whom are his business associates. I therefore request that he be removed from the committee to some other where his undoubted talents can be used to the advantage of the corporation."

My Lords, as a general rule English law gives effect to the ninth commandment that a man shall not speak evil falsely of his neighbour. It supplies a temporal sanction: if he cannot prove that defamatory matter which he published was true, he is liable in damages to whomever he has defamed, except where the publication is oral only, causes no damage and falls outside the categories of slander actionable per se. The public interest that the law should provide an effective means whereby a man can vindicate his reputation against calumny has nevertheless to be accommodated to the competing public interest in permitting

men to communicate frankly and freely with one another about matters in respect of which the law recognises that they have a duty to perform or an interest to protect in doing so. What is published in good faith on matters of these kinds is published on a privileged occasion. It is not actionable even though it be defamatory and turns out to be untrue. With some exceptions which are irrelevant to the instant appeal, the privilege is not absolute but qualified. It is lost if the occasion which gives rise to it is misused. For in all cases of qualified privilege there is some special reason of public policy why the law accords immunity from suit - the existence of some public or private duty, whether legal or moral, on the part of the maker of the defamatory statement which justifies his communicating it or of some interest of his own which he is entitled to protect by doing so. If he uses the occasion for some other reason he loses the protection of the privilege.

So, the motive with which the defendant on a privileged occasion made a statement defamatory of the plaintiff becomes crucial. The protection might, however, be illusory if the onus lay on him to prove that he was actuated solely by a sense of the relevant duty or a desire to protect the relevant interest. So he is entitled to be protected by the privilege unless some other dominant and improper motive on his part is proved. "Express malice" is the term of art descriptive of such a motive. Broadly speaking, it means malice in the popular sense of a desire to injure the person who is defamed and this is generally the motive which the plaintiff sets out to prove. But to destroy the privilege the desire to injure must be the dominant motive for the defamatory publication; knowledge that it will have that effect is not enough if the defendant is nevertheless acting in accordance with a sense of duty or in bona fide protection of his own legitimate interests.

The motive with which a person published defamatory matter can only be inferred from what he did or said or knew. If it be proved that he did not believe that what he published was true this is generally conclusive evidence of express malice, for no sense of duty or desire to protect his own legitimate interests can justify a man in telling deliberate and injurious falsehoods about another, save in the exceptional case where a person may be under a duty to pass on, without endorsing, defamatory reports made by some other person.

Apart from those exceptional cases, what is required on the part of the defamer to entitle him to the protection of the privilege is positive belief in the truth of what he published or, as it is generally though tautologously termed, "honest belief." If he publishes untrue defamatory matter recklessly, without considering or caring whether it be true or not, he is in this, as in other branches of the law, treated as if he knew it to be false. But indifference to the truth of what he publishes is not to be equated with carelessness, impulsiveness or irrationality in arriving at a positive belief that it is true. The freedom of speech protected by the law of qualified privilege may be availed of by all sorts and conditions of men. In affording to them immunity from suit if they have acted in good faith in compliance with a legal or moral duty or in protection of a legitimate interest the law must take them as it finds them. In ordinary life it is rare indeed for people to form their beliefs by a process of logical deduction from facts ascertained by a rigorous search for all available evidence and a judicious assessment of its probative value. In greater or in less degree according to their temperaments, their training, their intelligence, they are swayed by prejudice, rely on intuition instead of reasoning, leap to conclusions on inadequate evidence and fail to recognise the cogency of material which might cast doubt on the validity of the conclusions they reach. But despite the imperfection of the mental process by which the belief is arrived at it may still be "honest," that is, a positive belief that the conclusions they have reached are true. The law demands no more.

Even a positive belief in the truth of what is published on a privileged occasion - which is presumed unless the contrary is proved - may not be sufficient to negative express malice if it can be proved that the defendant misused the occasion for some purpose other than that for which the privilege is accorded by the law. The commonest case is where the dominant motive which actuates the defendant is not a desire to perform the relevant duty or to protect the relevant interest, but to give vent to his personal spite or ill will towards the person he defames. If this be proved, then even positive belief in the truth of what is published will not enable the defamer to avail himself of the protection of the privilege to which he would otherwise have been entitled. There may be instances of improper motives which destroy the privilege apart from personal spite. A defendant's dominant motive may have been to obtain some private advantage unconnected with the duty or the interest which constitutes the reason for the privilege. If so, he loses the benefit of the privilege despite his positive belief that what he said or wrote was true.

Judges and juries should, however, be very slow to draw the inference that a defendant was so far actuated by improper motives as to deprive him of the protection of the privilege unless they are satisfied that he did not believe that what he said or wrote was true or that he was indifferent to its truth or falsity. The motives with which human beings act are mixed. They find it difficult to hate the sin but love the sinner. Qualified privilege would be illusory, and the public interest that it is meant to serve defeated, if the protection which it affords were lost merely because a person, although acting in compliance with a duty or in protection of a legitimate interest, disliked the person whom he defamed or was indignant at what he believed to be that person's conduct and welcomed the opportunity of exposing it. It is only where his desire to comply with the relevant duty or to protect the relevant interest plays no significant part in his motives for publishing what he believes to be true that "express malice" can properly be found.

There may be evidence of the defendant's conduct upon occasions other than that protected by the privilege which justify the inference that upon the privileged occasion too his dominant motive in publishing what he did was personal spite or some other improper motive, even although he believed it to be true. But where, as in the instant case, conduct extraneous to the privileged occasion itself is not relied on, and the only evidence of improper motive is the content of the defamatory matter itself or the steps taken by the defendant to verify its accuracy, there is only one exception to the rule that in order to succeed the plaintiff must show affirmatively that the defendant did not believe it to be true or was indifferent to its truth or falsity. Juries should be instructed and judges should remind themselves that this burden of affirmative proof is not one that is lightly satisfied.

The exception is where what is published incorporates defamatory matter that is not really necessary to the fulfilment of the particular duty or the protection of the particular interest upon which the privilege is founded. Logically it might be said that such irrelevant matter falls outside the privilege altogether. But if this were so it would involve application by the court of an objective test of relevance to every part of the defamatory matter published on the privileged occasion; whereas, as everyone knows, ordinary human beings vary in their ability to distinguish that which is logically relevant from that which is not and few, apart from lawyers, have had any training which qualifies them to do so. So the protection afforded by the privilege would be illusory if it were lost in respect of any defamatory matter which upon logical analysis could be shown to be irrelevant to the fulfilment of the duty or the protection of the right upon which the privilege was founded. As Lord Dunedin pointed out in Adam v. Ward (1917) A.C. 309, 326-327 the proper rule as respects irrelevant defamatory matter incorporated in a statement made on a privileged occasion is to treat it as one of the factors to be taken into consideration in deciding whether, in all the circumstances, an inference that the defendant was actuated by express malice can properly be drawn. As regards irrelevant matter the test is not whether it is logically relevant but whether, in all the circumstances, it can be inferred that the defendant either did not believe it to be true or, though believing it to be true, realised that it had nothing to do with the particular duty or interest on which the privilege was based, but nevertheless seized the opportunity to drag in irrelevant defamatory matter to vent his personal spite, or for some other improper motive. Here, too, judges and juries should be slow to draw this inference.

My Lords, what is said by members of a local council at meetings of the council or of any of its committees is spoken on a privileged occasion. The reason for the privilege is that those who represent the local government electors should be able to speak freely and frankly, boldly and bluntly, on any matter which they believe affects the interests or welfare of the inhabitants. They may be swayed by strong political prejudice, they may be obstinate and pig-headed, stupid and obtuse; but they were chosen by the electors to speak their minds on matters of local concern and so long as they do so honestly they run no risk of liability for defamation of those who are the subjects of their criticism.

In the instant case Mr. Lowe's speech at the meeting of the Bolton Borough Council was upon matters which were undoubtedly of local concern. With one minor exception, the only facts relied upon as evidence from which express malice was to be inferred had reference to the contents of the speech itself, the circumstances in which the meeting of the council was held and the material relating to the subject matter of Mr. Lowe's speech which was within his actual knowledge or available to him on inquiry. The one exception was his failure to apologise to Mr. Horrocks when asked to do so two days later. A refusal to apologise is at best but tenuous evidence of malice, for it is consistent with a continuing belief in the truth of what one has said. Stirling J. found it to be so in the case of Mr. Lowe.

So the judge was left with no other material on which to found an inference of malice except the contents of the speech itself, the circumstances in which it was made and, of course, the defendant's own evidence in the witness box. Where such is the case the test of malice is very simple. It was laid down by Lord Esher himself, as Brett L.J., in Clark v. Molyneux, 3 Q.B.D. 237. It is: has it been proved that the defendant did not honestly believe that what he said was true, that is, was he either aware that it was not true or indifferent to its truth or falsity? In Royal Aquarium and Summer and Winter Garden Society Ltd. v. Parkinson (1892) 1 Q.B. 431 Lord Esher M.R. applied the self-same test. In the passage cited by Stirling J. he was doing no more than disposing of a suggestion made in the course of the argument that reckless disregard of whether what was stated was true or false did not constitute malice unless it were due to personal spite directed against the individual defamed. All Lord Esher M.R. was saying was that such indifference to the truth or falsity of what was stated constituted malice even though it resulted from prejudice with regard to the subject matter of the statement rather than with regard to the particular person defamed. But however gross, however unreasoning the prejudice it does not destroy the privilege unless it has this result. If what it does is to cause the defendant honestly to believe what a more rational or impartial person would reject or doubt he does not thereby lose the protection of the privilege.

I know of no authority which throws doubt upon this proposition apart from a Delphic dictum in the judgment of Greer L.J. in Watt v. Longsdon (1930) 1 K.B. 130, 154 where he gives as an example of a state of mind which constitutes malice: "A man may believe in the truth of a defamatory statement, and yet when he publishes it be reckless whether his belief be well founded or not." If "reckless" here means that the maker of the statement has jumped to conclusions which are irrational, reached without adequate inquiry or based on insufficient evidence, this is not enough to constitute malice if he nevertheless does believe in the truth of the statement itself. The only kind of recklessness which destroys privilege is indifference to its truth or falsity.

My Lords, in his judgment Stirling J. rejected the inference that Mr. Lowe was actuated by personal spite against Mr. Horrocks. He found, however, that Mr. Lowe was

"so anxious to have the plaintiff removed from the Management and Finance Committee that ... he did not consider fairly or objectively whether the evidence he had of the plaintiff's conduct over Bishops Road came anything like far enough to justify his conclusions or comments."

He then gave some examples of Mr. Lowe's jumping to conclusions and failing to make further inquiries and drew attention to his omission to refer to the dilemma in which Mr. Horrocks found himself vis-^-vis those who had purchased from his company building plots with the benefit of the restrictive covenant against building upon the land leased by the corporation to the Conservative Club.

It was no misuse of the occasion to use the Bishops Road fiasco in an attempt to obtain the removal of Mr. Horrocks from the Management and Finance Committee even though the prospects of success may have been slender until the balance of political power upon the council changed. The other matters referred to by the learned judge as showing Mr. Lowe to be grossly and unreasoningly prejudiced might have warranted the inference that he was indifferent to the truth or falsity of what he said if his own evidence as to his belief had been unconvincing. But it was an inference the judge, who heard and saw Mr. Lowe in the witness box, did not feel able to draw. "I am prepared," he said, "to accept what the defendant reiterated in his evidence that he believed and still believes that everything he said was true and justifiable, ..."

However prejudiced the judge thought Mr. Lowe to be, however irrational in leaping to conclusions unfavourable to Mr. Horrocks, this crucial finding of Mr. Lowe's belief in the truth of what he said upon that privileged occasion entitles him to succeed in his defence of privilege. The Court of Appeal so held. I would myself

do likewise and dismiss this appeal.

LORD KILBRANDON. My Lords, I have had the advantage of reading the speech which has been delivered by my noble and learned friend, Lord Diplock. For the reasons given by him, with which I agree, I would dismiss this appeal.

Appeal dismissed with costs.

Solicitors: Whitehouse, Gibson & Alton for Henry Fallows & Co., Bolton; Gregory, Rowcliffe & Co. for Woodcock & Sons, Bury.

Following an article I wrote in the Newton News 7.11.2006, Syd Howarth MBE the Editor wrote underneath it

" Editor. We have seen the documents to which Arun refers and can confirm their validity. Arun single handedly won a High Court case in London in 1999 against a team of Barristers and Solicitors,* winning commendations from Lord Justice Ward, Lord Justice Thorpe, Mr Justice Gage and Mr Justice Wilson,
When he was on the Town Council, his 8 inch thick dossier to the Councils solicitors was instrumental in getting a Defamation law suit against the late Cllr Tony Moore by the Woodham Golf & Country' Club dismissed."

(* Not reported but I have the transcript)

SOCIAL MEDIA: Think before you tweet!

The High Court in Cardiff has recently awarded damages to a Town Councillor after what is reported to be the first case in the UK where damages have been awarded for libel on social media website Twitter, Facebook etc. A defamatory statement is one which tends to lower the claimant in the estimation of right-thinking members of society generally. There are two types of defamation action – Libel and slander. Libel is the publication in permanent form of a defamatory statement 'written' whereas Slander is its publication in transitory form 'spoken'.

In an action for defamation, the Claimant must show that the words or comments made are defamatory, identify or refer to the Claimant and are published by the Defendant to a third party, i.e. posted on a social networking site.

Once the Claimant has proven these requirements, the Defendant in defending those proceedings would need to prove that the statement or comments made were true and therefore not defamatory or rely on another defamation defence such as fair comment or privilege.

In the recent case in the High Court in Cardiff, a Welsh Councillor agreed to pay damages of £3,000 after he published a false and defamatory statement on Twitter stating that a rival councillor had been removed from a polling station by the police during a by-election in 2009.
Both Councillors had been standing for election to Caerphilly County Council during which Colin Elsbury, the Plaid Cymru candidate, claimed on his Twitter page on the day of the poll: 'It's

not in our nature to deride our opponents however Eddie Talbot (an independent candidate), had to be removed by the Police from a polling station'. Mr Talbot argued that the statement was untrue and defamatory and Talbot said the statement left him open to ridicule.

At the hearing, Mr Elsbury reportedly agreed to pay Mr Talbot £3,000 in compensation and to publish an apology on Twitter. Mr Elsbury also agreed to pay Mr Talbot's legal costs which could run to several thousands of pounds resulting in a very expensive 'Tweet'.

It is clear from this case that the Courts will award damages for false and defamatory statements/'Tweets'/status updates posted on the various social networking sites such as Twitter and Facebook.

Councillors Right of Access to Information and Confidentiality

PART A. Access to Documents
1. RIGHTS UNDER THE 1985 ACT
In the main this Act gives greater rights to members of the public, and councillors obviously have these rights as have all people. Additionally, however, there are extra rights for councillors both specifically given and as a spin-off to the rights given to the public.
(i)   The Public's Rights
Under the Act the general public arc given the following rights:
(a)   to inspect and copy the agenda of any council, committee or sub-committee meeting three clear days before the meeting takes place
(b)   to inspect and copy any reports being considered during the public part of such a meeting
(c)   to inspect the minutes of any such meeting, although if the minutes of the private part of a meeting themselves reveal the information which led to the meeting being closed in the first place then only a summary giving a 'reasonably fair and coherent record' of the proceedings needs to be provided.
(d)   to inspect background papers used in the preparation of reports being discussed in public at any council, committee or sub-committee meetings.
However, background papers do not have to be made available if any part of these contain exempt or confidential information.
(ii)   Councillors' Additional Rights
The rights mentioned above are available to all members of the public including, therefore, councillors. However, elected members

are given some additional rights in Section IOOf of the Act. This states that a councillor may see any documents "in the possession or under the control" of the council which "contain material relating to any business to be transacted at a meeting of the council or a committee or sub-committee" unless those documents contain exempt information as defined in paragraphs 1-6.9,11,12 and 14 of Schedule 1. These rights thus apply to reports, minutes and background papers and they are wider than the public's rights in four important ways.

(a) The public's rights described above apply only to the public parts of meetings: thus for instance, background papers not themselves containing exempt information but relating to an agenda item that was being discussed in private

2. COMMON LAW RIGHTS: NEED TO KNOW

Although it has been repeatedly stated in various eases that "as to the right of a councillor to inspect all documents in possession of the council, there is no dispute", this does not give a member a right to a "roving commission" An idle curiosity is not a sufficient reason to inspect files the right exists "so far as his access to the documents is reasonably necessary to enable the councillor properly to perform his duties as a member of the council. The common law rights of a councillor to inspect documents ... arise from his common law duty to keep himself informed of all matters necessary to enable him properly to discharge his duties as a councillor" (R v Barnes Borough Council ex parte Conlan 1938 2 All E.R. 226). The judge in that case then went on to explain that these "duties are divided amongst various sub-committees" and thus a councillor is not "charged with the duty of making himself (sic) familiar with every document in the possession of the council". Thus the councillor's right to see documents, called by Lord Justice Donaldson in the Court of Appeal in the recent ease of R v Birmingham City Council ex parte O, the 'need to know' test, and now commonly referred to by that term, is based upon a need to know in order to enable the councillor to carry out his/her duties as a councillor. This is crucially important as will be seen below.

(I)   Need to know: Councillor on the relevant Committee

This is very straightforward and a councillor's rights arc very wide In the Birmingham City Council and O case (1983 1 A. (.579:1983 1 All E.R 497) referred to above. Lord Brightman was very explicit indeed in the case of a committee of which he is a member, a councillor as a general rule will ex hypothesis have good reason for access to all written material of such committee. So I do not doubt that each member of the social services committee is entitled by virtue of his office to see all the papers which have come into the possession of a social worker in the course of his duties as an employee of the council. There is no room for any secrecy as between a social worker and a member of the social services committee."

Thus in a case of a committee of which she is a member a councillor has access to all documents: whether relating to an item on the public or private part of an agenda; indeed even documents unrelated to actual agenda items (e.g. Where powers are delegated to officers, or simply matters being dealt with as day-to-day management/operational tasks) must be available. Even 'confidential' officers' working documents, as for example in the O case: "there is no room for any secrecy as between a social worker and a member of the social services committee Thus, w here a councillor is on the committee, the 'need to know' is very' wide and concerns all written material concerning the committee's functions.

(II)   Need to know: Sub-Committees

Suppose a councillor is on a parent committee that delegates certain of its functions to a sub-committee. How then does the need to know' principle apply to documents concerning matters being dealt with by the sub-committee? This matter was dealt with in the ease of R v Hackney Borough Council ex parte Gamper (1985 I W.L.R. 1229). As a member of the parent committee, the Public Services Committee. Cllr Gamper indicated a concern about matters coming before one of its subcommittees. the Direct Labour Organisation Sub-Committee, and sought both to

attend and observe meetings of that sub-committee (see page 16) and to be supplied with documents. The Council refused both. The court ruled that Cllr Gamper had a legitimate interest "as a member of the Public Services Committee which is the parent committee of the DLO Sub-Committee" and continued that "the committee...has residual responsibility for the matters delegated to the sub-committee and is answerable in its turn to the Council by virtue of its terms of reference. On this, if no other ground, he has demonstrated a 'need to know'". Furthermore, in the Gamper case the judge held that there was "no difference in principle" between a councillor asking for a single specified document and a councillor asking "for access to committee documents generally", once the 'need to know' has been demonstrated.

Another recent case on this matter is R v Sheffield City Council ex parte Chadwick (The Times 19.11.85). Cllr Chadwick, a member of the Policy Committee, was not a member of the Budget Sub-Committee established by that committee. He sought access to "all the relevant reports and papers associated with the 1985/6 Rate and Budget" claiming that "as an elected member of the Policy Committee I need to have information relating to how the Budget Sub-Committee will determine the 1985/6 Rate and Budget for the City." Although, as the judge stated, he was "undoubtedly provided with a considerable amount of financial information relevant to the making of a rate" including "a comprehensive report on the financial context together with details of the budget proposals of the controlling group1 which is the outcome of their deliberations in the sub-committee over many months" he was not given "the options which were considered by the Budget Sub- Committee." The Council argued that these were options being considered by the majority party (which made up the sub-committee) and were confidential, but apart from the court's ruling that it is unlawful to use a sub-committee as a party forum', the judge also found that Cllr Chadwick had a 'need to know' right of access to the relevant information: ' The need to know can, no doubt, be put on more than one basis but it is sufficient to say that in order to evaluate the recommendations of the sub-committee it was reasonable for Mr Chadwick to know what options had been considered before the recommended policy was chosen", and the judge held that "the committee and the Council could not reasonably take the view that he did not have a need to know. The budget proposals were one of the most important matters which the Policy Committee had to consider and any member of that committee is clearly concerned as to how any recommendations which he is invited to support came to be made."

This then has far reaching effects: councillors on a parent committee have a valid 'need to know' claim for documents listing options to enable them to evaluate recommendations. An additional significant factor in the Chadwick case was that, unlike the situation in the Gamper case, the Budget sub-committee had no delegated powers — it could only make recommendations that had to be approved by the Policy Committee. Nevertheless, Cllr Chadwick was deemed to have a need to know to enable him to evaluate the Sub-Committee's recommendations.

So what is the extent of the Gamper and Chadwick judgements as regards sub-committees? Do they give a councillor an automatic right to sec sub-committee documents if she is on a parent committee? The answer is probably not — quite. The judge in Gamper did at one point say that "there may be documents which are so confidential that they cannot be disclosed without passages being covered up or deleted". The test for that would have to be very high though, for as the judge said attend and observe meetings of that sub-committee Budget Sub-Committee will determine the 1985/6 Rate and Budget for the City." Although, as the judge stated, he was "undoubtedly provided with a considerable amount of financial information relevant to the making of a rate" including "a comprehensive report on the financial context together with details of the budget proposals of the controlling group which is the outcome of their deliberations in the sub-committee over many months"

This summarises the statutory right of access to information available to Councillors across the political spectrum in the UK. It is by no means exhaustive. All Councillors should be aware of who is fulfilling the "Monitoring Officer" role at their Council and this is the best person to ask regarding access to information and confidentiality.

Executive Summary

Councillors have the right to access any information held by the Council to which they are a member. Some information may be labelled "Confidential" but if that information would be accessible under the Freedom of Information Act then the Councillor is freely able to publish the information.

Summary
A Councillors right of access to information held by the Council to which they belong is derived from statute and case-law as follows;

Applying specifically to Councillors;
*   S.100F LGA 1972 and the Local Authorities (Executive Arrangements) (Access to Information) (England) Regulations 2000
*   The common law 'Need to Know'

Applying to all UK citizens;
*   The Freedom of Information Act 2000 and EI Regulations
*   S.17 Local Government and Finance Act 1982

COMMENT/NOTES: The right of access is NOT the same as the right to publish or otherwise make public. It is perfectly possible for a Councillor to be aware of something that they are unable to make public.

It is vitally important that when Councillors agree to be bound by Confidentiality Clauses in order to gain access to information they also make clear under what conditions the Confidentiality Clause comes to an end (typically the public disclosure of the information by the County Council or a third party where the County Council has publicly responded or is preparing to publicly respond to such a disclosure). The last thing Councillors need is to be effectively gagged by a confidentiality agreement when the information is already public!

The Right of a Councillor to access information is enshrined in the Local Government Act 1972, specifically (S.100(F) LGA 1972). This provides that any document held by the council containing material relating to any business to be transacted at any meeting of the council, committee or sub-committee working groups, must be available for inspection by any member of the council unless it is deemed by the proper officer to fall within certain categories of 'exempt' information (under Sched 12A), with the exception of para 3 (except to the extent that the information relates to proposed terms of a contract), and para 6.

Additionally there is a feature of Common Law called the 'Need to Know'. Under common law principles members of authorities have the right to access information held by the authority where it is reasonably necessary to enable the member to properly perform their duties as a councillor (Ex p Hook 1980). The House of Lords coined the phrase 'need to know' in a case involving a councillor who asked for access to a social services adoption file in order to assist in making an informed decision on a housing matter. The HL found that
even though the councillor wasn't a member of the social service committee they had established a bone fide need to know the information due to their role as a councillor.

In common with all citizens Councillors can also use the Freedom of information Act 2000 (FOI) and EI Regulations to access information. The General presumption is that information should be disclosed unless one of the exceptions contained in the act applies. The various exceptions include things such as legal privileged or commercially sensitive information.

Councillors have a statutory right to inspect any books, deeds, contracts, bills, vouchers and receipts prior to the annual audit

(Section 17, Local Government Finance Act, 1982). They also have a right to inspect accounts and to take copies throughout the year (Section 228(3), Local Government Act, 1972).

Confidentiality

Often administrations (of all political hues) will stamp the word "Confidential" on a document that for one reason or another they do not want to enter the public domain. Just because a document has the word "Confidential" on it it does not *always* mean that a Councillor in possession of the document is not able to make it public (of course some documents marked "Confidential" should remain confidential but it is based on the full content of the document, not just the use of the word Confidential!).

If the information is accessed using the FOI legislation, the information can be regarded as public i.e. the Councillor may share the information with others. In fact many Councils automatically disclose this information on their own websites.

However, if the Councillor has accessed information under the Common law 'Need to Know' power or under S.100F LGA 1972, in some cases the information will be 'confidential' in which case the Councillor will be bound by confidentiality.

If the Councillor accesses the information by any means other than FOI, they can check with the Monitoring Officer whether it is accessible by FOI. If the Monitoring Officer confirms that it is, then this supersedes any "confidential" markings on the papers, and the information can be used in public.

Working parties

It has been decided that local authorities have power to establish working parties (White Papers) to proffer advice to committees.' In R v Eden District Council, ex p Moffat,' councillor Moffat was excluded from the meetings of a working party which he claimed in fact was a sub-committee, and under SOs and common law he had a right to attend. On the facts, which included membership of the committee of chief officers,' it was held that the body was a working party, with consequently no right for Moffat to attend under the SOs.

Pursuant to the power in LGA 1972, s 111(1) and not under the exercise of functions through the council, committee, sub-committee or officers under s 101(1). The case concerned `confidential' items about appointments and restructuring. R v Eden District Council, ex- p Moffat (15 April 1987, unreported) CO/803 86; on appeal 8 November 1988 667/87 and (1988).

At first instance, Webster J believed that there was no reason in principle why a common law 'need to know' argument on behalf of a councillor could not be made out in relation to information before a working party of which s/he was not a member.' This, respectfully, must be correct, although in Moffat's case no need to know was established. **The fact that Moffat was a member of the council establishing the WP would have been influential, although membership of the parent will not confer automatic right of admission to its progeny.** His presence might inhibit frank discussion in a forum discussing tentatively provisional and sensitive matters, and he had no right to attend,' even though he may have benefited from being present in later council meetings discussing the report. Nourse L J on appeal believed this benefit constituted a 'need to know' and argued that a right to attend is not a right to participate, 'nor may it generally be objected that his presence there will inhibit others from speaking out as they would otherwise do' where he has a need to know. His right can only be defeated where his presence would cause injury to the public interest by eg breaching a confidence. 'It is not to be defeated by vague generalisations and the sensitivities of those who might feel more comfortable if he was excluded from their discussions'. **The two other judges did not believe there was a need to know, or a need to attend.'**

On appeal, Nourse L J agreed, Croom-Johnson Webster L J and Sir Denis Buckley J seemed not to, but Croom-Johnson Webster L J appeared to be arguing to the particular facts, not making a general principle. However, Webster L J at first instance believed the authority had acted unfairly and unlawfully in not allowing Moffat to explain why he had a bona fide right or need to attend. This refusal was unlawful, he held. **The Court of Appeal, however, did not agree. There was no right to attend, and therefore no right to explain why a right to attend might be established!**

In R v Sheffield City Council Ex parte Chadwick (1985) 84 LGR 563, the Divisional Court (Woolf J) took the view that it is not lawful for a council, by allowing a sub-committee to be used for party political purposes, to justify a need for confidentiality and secrecy which would not otherwise arise. However, it is not prima facie unlawful for a majority party to exclude members of other parties from committees. **If an excluded councillor reasonably requests information about committee meetings, the committee must provide that information, and if the most convenient way of supplying that information is by allowing him to attend the meeting, then he must be allowed to attend.** The position is of course different now with the need for political balance in committees and sub-committees arising out of the changes in s.15 and Schedule 15 of the Local Government and Housing Act 1989.

(not applying to Parish Councils)

In R v Hackney LBC Ex parte Gamper [1985] 1 W.L.R. 1229; [1985] 3 All E.R. 275; 83 L.G.R. 359; (1985) 82 L.S.G. 438 the Queen's Bench Division (Lloyd J) considered the case of G, the applicant, who was a Liberal councillor in the London Borough of Hackney, which had a large Labour majority. G was a member of both the public services committee and the housing sub-committee. The council was required by law to put its maintenance and construction work out to tender and to run its direct Labour organisations as a business. In this respect the public services committee appointed two sub-committees. **G was concerned about empty flats and inadequate repair services and sought access to meetings and agendas of the sub-committees, but was refused on the ground that they were confidential. G sought judicial review and the court held, in granting the application, that G needed access as a councillor, as a member of the housing sub-committee and of the public services committee in order to ensure that those committees were doing their work efficiently, in order to carry out his duties as a councillor. Furthermore, no reasonable council could properly have reached the decision to refuse such access, and the council's decisions would be quashed.**

If the council sets up a working party which is not a committee of that council a councillor who is not a working party member may find that his 'right to know' is out-weighed by other considerations such as the need for candid debate: R v EdenDistrict Council, ex p Moffat (1988). **However, a councillor's exclusion from a committee for party political purposes can never be legitimate: R v Sheffield CityCouncil, ex p Chadwick(1985).**

"Governance" in local authority terms means different things to different people. STANDARDS:

New measures, outlined in the Localism Act, replace the bureaucratic and controversial Standards Board regime, which minsters believe had become a system of nuisance complaints and petty, sometimes malicious, allegations of councillor misconduct that sapped public confidence in local democracy"

Localism Act 2011 ("the 2011 Act"). The 2011 Act, relevant parts of which came into force on 1 July 2012, abolished the local government standards framework established under the Local Government Act 2000, doing away with the Standards Board for England, the mandatory requirement on local authorities to have standards committees and the powers of the First Tier Tribunal to hear cases relating to local
government standards in England (powers formerly held by the Adjudication Panel for England).
In place of the old prescriptive regime, the 2011 Act imposed a general duty on local authorities to: "promote and maintain high standards of conduct by member and co-opted members of the authority" (s.27(1)). The legislation in its original form
removed entirely the requirement for local councils to maintain a code of conduct, intending to make it a voluntary matter, but amendments were introduced in the House of Lords requiring relevant authorities to adopt a code dealing with the conduct that is expected of members and co-opted members of the authority

when acting in that capacity (s.27(2)). The 2011 Act also introduced a new criminal offence of failing to declare or register a pecuniary interest (s.34) and made special provision in relation to allegations of predetermination or bias against local decision-makers (s.25).

These legislative changes (save in relation to predetermination) apply only to England (the provisions in relation to predetermination apply also to Wales): local

government standards are devolved to Scotland, Wales and Northern Ireland where different regimes apply. In Wales the standards regime under the Local Government Act 2000 has been retained.

Independent Persons

A major change, at least on its face, was the abolition of the obligation on local authorities to have standards committees chaired by an independent person. Under the 2011 Act relevant authorities are required to include in their procedures for determining allegations provision for the appointment of at least one "independent person" (s. 28(7)). The authority must seek, and take into account, the views of the independent person before it makes its decision on an allegation that it has decided to investigate, and it may seek his or her views in other circumstances.

Sanctions - a regime without teeth?

As to sanctions, under the new provisions there is no power to disqualify or suspend a local councillor for breach of an authority's code of conduct (the new criminal offence of failure to disclose a pecuniary interest may lead to disqualification as discussed below). The 2011 Act makes no provision as to what sanctions may be imposed pursuant to new locally devised procedures. However, absent express

statutory authority, a local authority could not lawfully grant itself the power to suspend democratically elected members.

In the recent case of Heesom v The Public Services Ombudsman for

Wales (2014)
EWHC 1504 (Admin) at (28), Hickinbottom J noted that:
It was uncontroversial before me that, there being no common law right for an authority to impose sanctions that interfere with local democracy, upon the abolition of these sanctions and outside the categories I have described above, a councillor in England can no longer be disqualified or suspended, sanctions being limited to (for example) a formal finding that he has breached the code, formal censure, press or other appropriate publicity, and removal by the authority from executive and committee roles (and then subject to statutory and constitutional requirements).

There have been reports in the media raising concerns about authorities powerless to prevent seriously discredited councillors from continuing to serve and claim their allowances. For example, Mid-Devon District Council were quoted recently as blaming the Localism Act for their inability to remove a councillor from office where the councillor had been convicted of benefit fraud.

The annual report of the Committee on Standards in Public Life (CSPL) 2013/14 stated that:
"the effectiveness of the sanctions regime for non-adherence to Local Authority codes of conduct, which apart from criminal prosecution, provides only for censure or suspension from a particular committee or committees, remains an issue of concern. We are aware that there have been recent individual cases that illustrate this, in particular the lack of a sanction to suspend councillors who have seriously breached the code of conduct."

In Practice
In these circumstances, the CSPL has emphasised the practical steps that authorities can and should take to promote high standards before any allegations arise, highlighting the importance of the Local Government Association (LGA) in
supporting strong leadership and the role of the LGA's peer challenge process in offering sector led improvement in this field. Another important area is training and induction: a majority of

councils offer induction for new elected members which covers their code of conduct and/or the "Nolan principles" of public life.

Registration of Interests

Where the 2011 Act has more teeth is in relation to the registration of interests. A member or co-opted member of a relevant authority must, within 28 days of taking office, notify the authority's monitoring officer of any disclosable pecuniary
interests (s.30). A member may not, in general, participate in any discussion or vote in which he has a pecuniary interest (s.31) (although dispensation to participate may be granted in certain limited circumstances (s.33)). Disclosable pecuniary interests are listed under schedule 2 of the Relevant Authorities (Disclosable Pecuniary Interests) Regulations 2012.
It is a criminal offence if a member or co-opted member, without reasonable excuse, fails to comply with these requirements (s.34). The offences are punishable by a fine
of up to level 5 (currently £5,000) and an order disqualifying the person from being, or becoming, a member or co-opted member of a relevant local authority for up to five years.

Predetermination and Bias

The 2011 Act also addresses the circumstances in which a decision may be quashed where it is alleged that a councillor was biased. The relevant provision is section 25 which states:
(1) Subsection (2) applies if—
(a) as a result of an allegation of bias or predetermination, or otherwise, there is an issue about the validity of a decision of a relevant authority, and
 (b) it is relevant to that issue whether the decision-maker, or any of the decision-makers, had or appeared to have had a closed mind (to any extent) when making the decision.
 (2) A decision-maker is not to be taken to have had, or to have appeared to have had, a closed mind when making the decision just

because—

(a) the decision-maker had previously done anything that directly or indirectly indicated what view the decision-maker took, or would or might take, in relation to a matter, and

(b) the matter was relevant to the decision.

The intention of this provision, as described in the Explanatory Notes, is to clarify the common law on how the concept of 'predetermination' applies to councillors in England and Wales:

"The section makes it clear that if a councillor has given a view on an issue, this does not show that the councillor has a closed mind on that issue, so that that if a councillor has campaigned on an issue or made public statements about their approach to an item of council business, he

or she will be able to participate in discussion of that issue in the council and to vote on it if it arises in an item of council business requiring a decision."

This section has been cited by local authority defendants in a number of recent judicial review claims. In I.M. Properties Development Ltd v Taylor Wimpey Ltd (2014) EWHC 2440 (Admin), Patterson J confirmed that the provision is not limited to public statements and that it may cover the sending of an e-mail.

The courts have repeatedly held that the public expression of a preference by an elected member does not constitute predetermination (see, R (Island Farm Development Ltd) v Bridgend County BC (2006) EWHC Admin 2189;

R (Lewis) v Redcar & Cleveland BC (2008) EWCA Civ 746); and the words "just because" in section 25 leave scope for a court to find that there was predetermination where a local authority decision maker has expressed a view on a matter and other factors are present to demonstrate a closed mind.

THE CONDUCT OF MEETINGS

24. Where councils are the decision-maker, the usual practice is to

have the important documents which need to be considered available to the Councillors, for example in a file or on a table in the council chamber or room where the decision is being considered and taken. To what extent must officers ensure that the councillors have actually read the material which the Council is required to take into account? There have been a number of cases recently on the conduct of local
authority meetings, and whether sufficient information was put before the meeting.

Materials available to meeting:

R (Hunt) v North Somerset Council
The first is the Court of Appeal's decision in R (Hunt) v North Somerset Council (2014) LGR 1. The case concerned a challenge to an item in a local authority's budget, and the decision-making undertaken to reach that budgetary decision. The principal ground of challenge was the now familiar public sector equality duty challenge, under section 149 of the Equality Act 2010, i.e. alleging that the local authority has not paid due regard to equality issues when making its decision. The specific issue that arose here was the extent to which it must be proven that decision-makers have personally read information prepared by officers on equalities impacts. The local authority had proposed to reduce its spending on youth services by around £365,000 for the financial year. It published the proposal on its website and in its own monthly magazine; and it held meetings with representatives of local youth clubs.

The local authority also updated its Equality Impact Assessments (EIAs), one of which applied solely to the impact of budget reduction proposals in relation to services for children and young persons. However only summaries of the EIAs were put before council members in advance of the meeting at which a final decision was made to approve the cuts. Councillors were told how to access the full EIAs in an
appendix to the document that they received, but they were not

specifically directed to consider them.

Section 507B of the Education 1996 Act requires LAs to "take steps to ascertain the views of qualifying young persons in (its) area". The appellant was a 22 year old with ADHD, learning difficulties and behavioural problems, and as such was a "qualifying young person". The Court of Appeal held that there was "not sufficient evidence" to conclude that the local authority had taken the required steps. As to the equality duty, the Court of Appeal crucially rejected the argument (accepted at first instance) that it could be inferred that council members had considered the full EIAs. **The Court held that "if council members are provided with a particular set of materials for the purpose of a meeting, they can, absent positive evidence to the contrary effect, be taken to have read all such materials and also to have read any additional materials to which they were expressly referred".**

However that was not the case here. The report to the Councillors who made the decision did not indicate "any need or requirement to read the EIAs themselves. Whilst they were told how to access the EIAs, they were not told, either expressly or impliedly, that they must or should consider them before the meeting". The failure of the decision-makers to consider the full EIAs breached the PSED. Despite this the Court of Appeal refused to grant any relief. The decision could not be quashed without also quashing the Council's decision to approve the entire revenue budget for 2012/2013. It was too late to unwind what had already been done and to grant relief in these circumstances would be "detrimental to good administration".

Comments: This decision affirms that general practice of having important documents which need to be considered available to the Councillors, though highlights the crucial importance of officers drawing attention in sufficiently clear terms to the need to actually read that material.

It should also be noted this practice only gives rise to a presumption that the necessary materials have in fact been considered. Such a presumption can be rebutted. For example, a dissenting councillor may sign a witness statement claiming that

throughout the decision-making meeting the file containing the necessary reading was not opened. **Local authorities need to be wary of such problems, and take steps as far as they are able to ensure that Councillors actually read the materials prepared for them.** This is particularly the case where such materials relate to a statutory mandatory consideration, such as the PSED.

Breach of publication requirements: R (Joicey) v Northumberland CC R (Joicey) v Northumberland CC (2014) EWHC 3657 concerned the effect of breaches of requirements to publish information in advance of meetings at which decisions are made, and the effect of such breaches.

The case concerned a planning application for a wind turbine. Noise was a key issue in the application, and the local authority had commissioned a noise report.

Sections 100A-E of the Local Government Act 1972 provide for rights to access to local authority meetings. Section 100B provides for access to agendas and reports.

Section 100D provides for access to background papers. All such documents must be "open to inspection by members of the public at the offices of the council" at least five clear days before the meeting. In this case the noise report, a key background paper within section 100D of the 1972 Act, was not available for inspection for the required five clear days before the meeting. One of the people opposing the planning application became aware of the existence of a noise report. He requested to see a copy of the report before the meeting. He also attended the Council offices to inspect the files, but did not find any noise report there.

The day before the meeting the noise report was uploaded to the Council website and was also, separately, provided to the person who had requested it. **Mr Joicey attended the Council committee meeting and complained about the fact that it had appeared only the day before. He later brought judicial review proceedings, raising the non-availability of the noise report as one of his grounds. The Court held that there had been a number of** breaches of the public's right to information under the Local Government Act 1972. Further, the fact that the report was not available on the Council's website also constituted a breach of its undertakings in its Statement of Community Involvement, prepared pursuant to its obligations under section 18 of the Planning and Compulsory Purchase Act 2004. The local authority urged the Court to decline relief, on the basis that the local authority said it was inevitable that the same result would have been reached regardless of this breach. The Court was unwilling to accept that argument. Relief would only be refused on such a basis if the Court decided that the result would inevitably have been the same, and the Court was unable to find that the decision would inevitably have been the same if the noise report had been made available earlier. The planning permission was quashed.

TRANSPARENCY AND ACCOUNTABILITY

In October 2014 the DCLG issued the Local Government Transparency Code 2014
("the Code"). It deals with the publication by local authorities of information relating to the discharge of their functions.
The Code was issued pursuant to section 2 of the Local Government, Planning and Land Act 1980.
The stated purposes of the Code are to "place more power into citizens' hands to increase democratic accountability and make it easier for local people to contribute to the local decision making process" (Code para 1). The Code's starting position is stark: "all data held and managed by local authorities should be made available to local people unless there are specific sensitivities" (Code para 3).
Part 2 of the Code then lists types of information and publication cycles. All expenditure over £500 and procurement information, are to be published quarterly: Code paras 21-22.
Various types of information relating to local authority land holdings, parking, senior salaries and a variety of other organisational information, are to be published annually: see Part

2.2 of the Code. Details of waste contracts need only be published once: para 44. Part 3 of the Code goes into more detail on the minimum data that should be published under each category. These provisions are expressed as "recommendations".

The Local Audit and Accountability Act 2014

This abolished the Audit Commission and establishes new arrangements for the audit and accountability of local public bodies, including certain health service bodies that were previously audited by the Audit Commission. The main changes brought about by the Act are -

Abolition of the Audit Commission as mentioned, and transfer of its continuing functions to other bodies.

A requirement for relevant authorities to keep accounting records and to prepare an annual statement of accounts, which must be audited. A requirement to appoint an external and independent auditor and to publish

information about the appointment. A requirement that an audit must include a value for money element. The creation of a regulatory framework for local audit, by which the Financial

Reporting Council and professional accountancy bodies regulate the provision of local audit services.

The transfer of responsibility for setting the code of audit practice and supporting guidance to the National Audit Office.

A power for the Secretary of State to commission an inspection of a best value authority.

A new regulation-making power to enable the Secretary of State to make regulations to allow the public to film, blog and tweet at the public meetings of local government bodies.

Guidance issued by DCLG
states that the member does not have to differentiate between their own or their spouse/civil partner/partners interests or to name them:
Does my spouse's or civil partner's name need to appear on

the register of interests?

No. For the purposes of the register, an interest of your spouse or civil partner, which is listed in the national rules, is your disclosable pecuniary interest. Whilst the detailed format of the register of members' interests is for your council to decide, there is no requirement to differentiate your disclosable pecuniary interests between those which relate to you personally and those that relate to your spouse or civil partner.

Dispensations

Councillors may apply to the council for a 'dispensation' to allow them to take part in a debate from which they would otherwise be debarred by the nature of their pecuniary interests. A dispensation may be granted for any reason, but the Act specifies a number of scenarios in which this may be done: this includes so many councillors having interests that the meeting cannot proceed, or the political balance of the meeting being substantially affected. A dispensation may last for a maximum of four years.

Guidance published in September 2013 clarified that owning a property in the local authority area does not constitute a disclosable pecuniary interest for the purposes of setting council tax.8 Councillors owning property in the council area would be expected to declare this as an interest, but it is not a disclosable pecuniary interest. Therefore a councillor is not prevented from taking part in a debate on that issue, nor would they need to seek a dispensation from the council to take part. Nevertheless, some councils have granted four-year dispensations on this point, to ensure compliance with the 2011 Act.

Nolan Principles in Public Life

1. Selflessness

Holders of public office should act solely in terms of the public interest.

2. Integrity

Holders of public office must avoid placing themselves under any obligation to people or organisations that might try inappropriately to influence them in their work. They should not act or take decisions in order to gain financial or other material benefits for themselves, their family, or their friends. They must declare and resolve any interests and relationships.

3. Objectivity

Holders of public office must act and take decisions impartially, fairly and on merit, using the best evidence and without discrimination or bias.

4. Accountability

Holders of public office are accountable to the public for their decisions and actions and must submit themselves to the scrutiny necessary to ensure this.

5. Openness

Holders of public office should act and take decisions in an open and transparent manner. Information should not be withheld from the public unless there are clear and lawful reasons for so doing.

6. Honesty

Holders of public office should be truthful.

7. Leadership

Holders of public office should exhibit these principles in their own behaviour. They should actively promote and robustly support the principles and be willing to challenge poor behaviour wherever it occurs.

DURHAM COUNTY COUNCIL PROCEDURE FOR LOCAL ASSESSMENT OF COMPLAINTS

1. The Localism Act 2011 requires that the Council adopt arrangements for dealing with complaints of breach of the Code of Conduct both by Council members and Parish Council members.

The Council's Monitoring Officer will seek to resolve complaints swiftly to the satisfaction of the complainant using local resolution whenever possible. Complaints will only be referred for local investigation as a last resort in view of the

disproportionate amount of time involved and the limited sanctions available to the Standards Committee under the new legislation.

Any person may make a written complaint to the Council's Monitoring Officer alleging that a councillor has acted in breach of the Code of Conduct for Members.

Any such complaint should be sent using the Complaint Form to

the Monitoring Officer, Durham County Council County Hall Durham, DH1 5UL

The following procedure will normally be followed on receipt of such a complaint. This procedure should be read in conjunction with the Council's Local Determination Procedure.

2. Initial Notification of Complaint

2.1 Unless paragraph 2.2 applies the member who is the subject of the complaint will as soon as practicable after the complaint is received be informed in writing by the Monitoring Officer of the nature of complaint, which paragraphs of the Code of Conduct have been allegedly breached and (unless the complainant has requested and been granted anonymity) the name of the complainant.

2.2 The Monitoring Officer may withhold this information from the member subject of the complaint if s/he considers that disclosure would be against the public interest or might prejudice any future investigation, or where non-disclosure has been specifically requested by the complainant for what the Monitoring Officer considers may be good reasons.

2.3 The Monitoring Officer, in consultation with the Independent Person may apply the Habitual or Vexatious Complaints Policy at Appendix 2 to a complaint where appropriate.

3. Initial Assessment

3.1 The Monitoring Officer, in consultation with the Independent person where appropriate, will as soon as reasonable, and normally within 20 working days of

receipt of the complaint, consider and decide if any action should be taken on it. The Assessment Criteria contained in Appendix 3 will be applied.

3.2 The Monitoring Officer will decide either:

(a) That no action should be taken in respect of it

(b) To seek local resolution

(c) To refer the complaint for investigation

(d) To refer the complaint to the Standards Committee Reports/Local Assessment 3

3.3 Where the complaint is against a person who is no longer a Member of the Council, but is a member of another relevant authority, the Monitoring Officer may instead refer the complaint to the Monitoring officer of that other relevant authority if s/he thinks it more appropriate to do so.

3.4 After making the decision, the Monitoring Officer will produce a written summary of the decision which will include the main points considered, the conclusion and the

reasons for that conclusion. The summary will be sent as soon as possible to the complainant and to the Member who is the subject of the complaint.

That summary will be available for inspection at the offices of the Council for 6 years beginning with the date of the decision. However, the summary will not be made available for inspection, until the member who was the subject of the complaint has received a written summary of the decision.

3.5 A written summary of the decision will also be sent to the clerk of the relevant

parish/town council where applicable.

4. No action to be taken in respect of the complaint

4.1 Where the Monitoring Officer decides that no further action is warranted in relation to the complaint, the complaint will be closed and there is no appeal process.

5. Local Resolution

5.1 The Monitoring Officer will establish whether a complaint is suitable to be resolved informally before taking a decision on whether the complaint merits formal investigation. This may involve

a) Exploring whether the member is prepared to apologise for the act or omission complained of;

b) Arranging for the Member who is the subject of the complaint to attend a training course;

c) Arranging for that Member and the complainant to engage in a process of conciliation;

d) Such other steps (not including an investigation), as appear appropriate to the Monitoring Officer.

6. Referral by Monitoring Officer for investigation

6.1 Where the Monitoring Officer refers the complaint for investigation, the procedure set out in paragraph 6.3 below will apply.

6.2 The Monitoring Officer may reconsider the complaint at any time if:

(a) As a result of new evidence or information presented by the Investigating Officer,

s/he is of the opinion:

(i) The matter is materially more or less serious than may have seemed apparent when the s/he referred it for investigation and

(ii) The Monitoring Officer would have made a different decision had s/he been aware of that new evidence or information; OR Reports/Local Assessment 4

(b) The person who is the subject of the complaint has died; or is seriously ill; or has resigned from the Council, and the Monitoring Officer considers that in the circumstances it is no longer appropriate to continue with an investigation.

6.3 If a matter is referred back to the Monitoring Officer, s/he will reconsider and make one of the decisions set out in paragraph 3.2 above.

In forming an opinion for the purposes of paragraph 6.2(a) above, the Monitoring Officer may take account of:

(a) The failure of any person to co-operate with an investigation; OR

(b) An allegation that the Member concerned has engaged in a further breach of the Council's Code of Conduct or that of another relevant authority; OR

(c) An allegation that another member has engaged in a related breach of the Council's Code of Conduct or that of another relevant authority.

6.4 Where the investigation finds evidence of a failure to comply with the Code of Conduct, the Monitoring Officer, in consultation with the Independent person, may seek local resolution to the satisfaction of the complainant in appropriate cases.

Where such local resolution is not appropriate or possible the investigation findings will be reported to a Hearings Panel of the Standards Committee for local determination.

6.5 A Hearing Panel shall, in the absence of good reason to the contrary, be convened within three months of the completion of the Investigating Officer's report to hear and determine any allegation that a Councillor has failed or may have failed to comply with the Code of Conduct for Members. The procedure for Hearing Panels contained in the Local Determinations Procedure shall be complied with.

The Hearing Panel shall comprise three Members of the Standards Committee selected by the Monitoring Officer. A quorum of the Hearing Panel will be three Members.

6.6 The Hearing Panel shall make one of the following findings, namely:-

(a) That the Member who was the subject of the Hearing had not failed to comply with the Code of Conduct of any authority concerned; or

(b) That the Member who was the subject of the Hearing had failed to comply with the Code of Conduct of an authority concerned, but that no action needs to be taken in respect of the matters which were considered at the Hearing; or

(c) That the Member who was the subject of the Hearing had failed to comply with the Code of Conduct of an authority concerned and that action should be taken.

7. Decision to take no action in respect of allegation

7.1 If the Hearing Panel decides that no action should be taken in respect of the complaint, it must take reasonable steps to give written notice of the decision and the reasons for it to:

(a) The complainant;

(b) The person who was the subject of the complaint; AND Reports/Local Assessment

(c) The clerk of the relevant parish/town Council where applicable It shall endeavour to send this notice within 5 working days of the Hearing Panel's decision.

8. Withdrawing Complaints

8.1 If a complainant requests to withdraw his/her complaint before the Monitoring Officer

has made a decision on it, then the Monitoring Officer will decide whether to grant that request.

In making that decision s/he will take into account the following considerations:

• Does the public interest in taking some action on the complaint outweigh the complainant's desire to withdraw it?

• Is the complaint such that action can be taken on it, for example, an investigation without the complainant's participation?

• Is there an identifiable underlying reason for the request to withdraw the complaint? For example, is there information to suggest that the complainant may have been pressured by the

member who is the subject of the complaint,
or an associate of theirs, to withdraw the complaint?

Your address and contact details will not usually be released unless necessary or to deal with your complaint.

However, we will tell the following people that you have made this complaint: the member(s) you are complaining about

any other person whom we consider it necessary to inform to properly investigate your complaint.

We will tell them your name and give them a summary of your complaint. We will give them full details of your complaint where necessary or appropriate to be able to deal with it. If you have serious concerns about your name and a summary, or details, of your complaint being released, please complete section 6 of the form.

Please tell us which complainant type best describes you:

Member of the public

An elected or co-opted member of an authority

Member of Parliament

Local authority monitoring officer

Other council officer or authority employee Reports/Local Assessment

Equality monitoring questions

We have attached an Equality Monitoring Form to the back of this complaint form which you are invited to complete as well.

Making your complaint

Your complaint will initially be considered, usually within 20 working days, by the Council's Monitoring Officer, in consultation with the Independent Person if appropriate. The Monitoring Officer will decide whether any action should be taken on your complaint. You will be advised of that decision. If the decision is to take action, the Monitoring Officer can appoint an Investigating Officer to investigate the

complaint. If your complaint is investigated and a breach of the Code of Conduct is found, the result will be reported to a Hearing Panel of the Council's Standards Committee which will then decide if there has been a breach of the Members' Code of Conduct and, if so, what action to take.

Please provide us with the name of the member(s) you believe have breached the Code of Conduct and the name of the authority of which they are a member Title First name Last name Council or authority name 5. Please explain in this section (or on separate sheets) what the member has done

which you believe breaches the Code of Conduct. If you are complaining about more than one member you should clearly explain what each individual person has done which you believe breaches the Code of Conduct.

It is important that you provide all the information you wish to have taken into account by the assessment sub-committee when it decides whether to take any action on your complaint.

For example: You should be specific, wherever possible; about exactly what you are alleging the member said or did. For instance, instead of writing that the member insulted you, you should state what it was they said. You should provide the dates of the alleged incidents wherever possible. If you cannot provide exact dates it is important to give a general timeframe. You should explain whether there are any witnesses to the alleged conduct and provide their names and contact details if possible. You should provide any relevant background information

Please provide us with the details of your complaint. Continue on a separate sheet if there is not enough space on this form.

Only complete this next section if you are requesting that your identity or details of your complaint is kept confidential

In the interests of fairness and natural justice, we believe members who are complained about have a right to know who has made the complaint. We also believe they have a right to be provided with a summary of the complaint and then further details of it if there is a decision to investigate it or take other action on it.

We will not withhold your identity, or a summary or the details of your complaint, unless you have exceptional reasons why we should do so.

If you think you have such reasons and want us to consider withholding your identity and/or any details of your complaint, either altogether or for some period of time, you
must cross out the statement in the box below giving your consent to such disclosure. You must also attach to this form a separate sheet which fully explains what information you want withheld and your reasons for your request to withhold it.

I understand and agree that my name and details of this complaint will be disclosed to the persons mentioned in paragraph 1 above. If you do request confidentiality and this is not granted, we will usually allow you the option of withdrawing your complaint.

However, it is important to understand that in certain exceptional circumstances where the matter complained about is very serious, we may still proceed with an investigation or other action and disclose your name even if you have expressly asked us not to.

Additional Help

Complaints must be submitted in writing. This includes fax and email submissions. However, in line with the requirements of the Disability Discrimination Act 2000, we can make reasonable adjustments to assist you if you have a disability that prevents you from making your complaint in writing.

If you need any support in completing this form, please let us know as soon as possible. You should initially contact the Council's Monitoring Officer who will try to arrange appropriate assistance for you.

Habitual or Vexatious Complaints Policy

1. Introduction

1.1.1 This policy identifies situations where complainants, either individually or as part of a group, or a group of complainants, might be considered to be "habitual or vexatious" and ways of responding to these situations.

1.1.2 This policy is intended to assist in identifying and managing persons who seek to be disruptive to the Monitoring Officer through pursuing an unreasonable course of conduct.

1.2 In this policy:

Habitual means: done repeatedly or as a habit. Vexatious means: an action brought for the purpose of annoying the opponent and with no reasonable prospect of success.

1.4 Habitual or vexatious complaints can be a problem for officers and Members. The difficulty in handling such complaints is that they are time consuming and wasteful of

resources in terms of officer and member time and displace scarce human resources that could otherwise be spent on council priorities. Whilst the Monitoring Officer endeavours to process all complaints under the local assessment procedure there are times when there is nothing further which can reasonably be done to assist or to rectify a real or perceived problem.

2. Habitual or Vexatious Complainants

2.1 For the purpose of this policy, the following definition of habitual or vexatious complainants will be used:

The repeated and/or obsessive pursuit of:

(i) Unreasonable complaints and/or unrealistic outcomes; and/or

(ii) Reasonable complaints in an unreasonable manner.

2.2 Prior to considering its implementation, the Monitoring Officer will send a summary of this policy to the complainant to give them prior notification of its possible implementation.

2.3 Where complaints continue and have been identified as habitual or vexatious in accordance with the criteria set out in Schedule A, the Monitoring Officer will consult with the Independent Person to seek agreement to treat the complaint as habitual or vexatious and for an appropriate course of action to be taken. Schedule B details the options available for dealing with habitual or vexatious complaints.

2.4 The Monitoring Officer will notify complainants, in writing of the reasons why their complaint has been treated as habitual or vexatious and the action that will be taken.

The Monitoring Officer will also notify the Ward Member that a constituent has been designated as a habitual and vexatious complainant to Standards Committee.

2.5 Once a complainant has been determined to be habitual or vexatious, their status will be kept under review after one year and monitored by the Monitoring Officer with reports being taken to Standards Committee as required. If a complainant
subsequently demonstrates a more reasonable approach then their status will be reviewed.

Schedule A - Criteria for determining habitual or vexatious complainants

Complainants (and/or anyone acting on their behalf) may be deemed to be habitual or vexatious where previous or current contact with them shows that they meet one of the following criteria. Where complainants:

1) Persist in pursuing a complaint where the local assessment process has been fully and properly implemented and exhausted.

2) Persistently change the substance of a complaint or frequently raise new issues or seek to prolong contact by frequently raising further concerns or questions whilst the complaint is being addressed. (Care must be taken however not to disregard new issues which are significantly different from the original complaint as they need to be addressed as a separate complaint.)

3) Are repeatedly unwilling to accept documented evidence given as being factual or deny receipt of an adequate response in spite of correspondence specifically answering their questions or do not accept that facts can sometimes be difficult to verify after a long period of time has elapsed.

4) Repeatedly do not clearly identify the precise issues which they wish to complain about despite reasonable efforts of officers to help them specify their concerns and/or where the concerns identified do not fall within the remit of the local assessment process.

5) Regularly focus on a trivial matter to an extent which is out of proportion to its significance and continue to focus on this point. It is recognised that determining what a trivial matter is can be subjective and careful judgement
will be used in applying this criteria.

6) Has threatened or used physical violence towards employees at

any time.

This will itself cause personal contact with the complainant and/or their representative to be discontinued and the complaint will, therefore, only be continued to be written communication. The Council must determine that any

complainant who threatens or uses actual physical violence towards employees will be regarded as a vexatious complainant. The complainant will be informed of this in writing together with notification of how future contact

with the Council is to be made.

7) Have in the course of addressing a complaint to the Monitoring Officer had an excessive number of contacts with the Council, placing unreasonable demands on officers. A contact may be made in person by telephone, letter, email or fax. Judgment will be used to determine excessive contact taking into account a specific circumstance of each individual case.

8) Have harassed or been verbally abusive on more than one occasion towards officers dealing with complaints. Officers recognise that complainants may sometimes act out of character in times of stress, anxiety or distress and will make reasonable allowances for this. Some complainants may have a mental health disability and there is a need to be sensitive in circumstances of that kind.

9) Are known to have recorded meetings or face to face/telephone conversations without prior knowledge and consent by the parties involved.

10) Make unreasonable demands on the Council and its employees and fail to accept these may be unreasonable, for example insist on an action being

taken by Standards Committee which falls outside of its remit. 11) Make unreasonable complaints which impose a significant burden on the human resources of the Council and where the complaint:

Clearly does not have any serious purpose or value; or

Is designed to cause disruption or annoyance; or

Has the effect of harassing the Council; or Can otherwise fairly be characterized as obsessive or manifestly unreasonable

12) Make repetitive complaints and allegations which ignore the replies which the Council has supplied in previous correspondence

Schedule B - Options for dealing with habitual or vexatious complainants

The options below can be used singularly or in combination depending on the circumstances of the case and whether the complaint is ongoing or completed.

1) A letter to the complainant setting out responsibilities for the parties involved if the Monitoring Officer is going to assess the complaint. If terms are contravened, consideration will then be given to implementing other action as indicated below.

2) Decline any contact with the complainant, either in person, by telephone, by fax, by letter, by email or any combination of these provided that one form of contact is maintained. This may also mean that only one named officer will be nominated to maintain contact and the complainant is notified of this
person.

3) Notify the complainant in writing, that the Council has responded fully to the points raised and has tried to resolve the complaint but there is nothing more to add and continuing contact on the matter will serve no useful purpose. The
complainant will also be notified that the correspondence is at an end, advising the complainant that they are being treated as a habitual or vexatious complainant and as such the Council does not intend to engage in further correspondence dealing with the complaint.

Assessment Criteria

The following criteria will be taken into account in deciding what action, if any, to take:

1. Has the complainant submitted enough information to satisfy the Monitoring Officer that the complaint should be referred for investigation? If not, the information provided is insufficient. The only outcome can be that no further action is taken on the

complaint and a decision notice to that effect will be issued accordingly.

2. Is the complaint about someone who is no longer a Member of the Council, but is a Member of another authority? If so, does the Monitoring Officer wish to refer the complaint to the Monitoring Officer of that other authority?

If yes, the complaint will be referred to the Monitoring Officer of that other authority to consider if he/she thinks it more appropriate to do so.

3. Has the complaint already been the subject of an investigation or other action relating to the Code of Conduct in the last 3 years? Similarly, has the complaint been the subject of an investigation by other regulatory authorities in the last 3 years? If yes, there may be nothing more to be gained by further action being taken.

4. Is the complaint about something which happened so long ago that there would be little benefit in taking action now?

If yes, further action will not normally be warranted.

5. Does the complaint appear too trivial to justify the cost or inconvenience of investigation?

If yes, investigation will not be warranted.

6. Does the complaint appear to be simply malicious, politically motivated or tit-for-tat? If yes, further action will not normally be warranted.

7. Is the complaint anonymous?

If yes, no action will normally be taken, unless there are compelling reasons to suggest otherwise. For example, if it includes documentary evidence or photographic evidence

indicating an exceptionally serious or significant matter.

Councillors note that if told you that you have no right of appeal. Everyone has recourse to the High Court   see pages 70, 82, 134.

Waiver of 6 month Councillor attendance rule (Section 85 Local Government Act 1972).

Section 85 (1) of the Local Government Act 1972 requires a member of a Local Authority to attend at least one meeting of that Authority within a six month consecutive period, in order to avoid being disqualified as a Councillor. This requirement can be waived and the time limit extended if any failure to attend was due to a reason approved by the Authority, in advance of the six month period expiring. A formal request has to be made for an extension to the six month rule to be approved.

Section 85 (1) of the Local Government Act 1972 states that "if a member of a Local Authority fails, throughout a period of six consecutive months from the date of their last attendance, to attend any meeting of the Authority they will, unless the failure was due to some good reason approved by the Authority before the expiry of that period, cease to be a member of the Authority." Attendance can be at any committee or sub-committee, or any joint committee, joint board or other body where the functions of the Authority are discharged or who were appointed to advise the Authority on any matter relating to the discharge of their functions. A Council can only consider approval of any reasons for non-attendance before the end of the relevant six month period.

Once any councillor loses office, through failure to attend for the six month period, the disqualification cannot be overcome by the councillor subsequently resuming attendance nor can retrospective approval of the Council be sought for an extension in time.

Misconduct in Public Office

Misconduct in public office is an offence at common law triable only on indictment. It carries a maximum sentence of life imprisonment. It is an offence confined to those who are public office holders and is committed when the office holder acts (or fails to act) in a way that constitutes a breach of the duties of that office.

The Court of Appeal has made it clear that the offence should be strictly confined. It can raise complex and sometimes sensitive issues. Prosecutors should therefore consider seeking the advice of the Principal Legal Advisor to resolve any uncertainty as to whether it would be appropriate to bring a prosecution for such an offence.

Where there is clear evidence of one or more statutory offences, they should usually form the basis of the case, with the 'public office' element being put forward as an aggravating factor for sentencing purposes.

The decision of the Court of Appeal in Attorney General's Reference No 3 of 2003 (2004) EWCA Crim 868 does not go so far as to prohibit the use of misconduct in public office where there is a statutory offence available. There is, however, earlier authority for preferring the use of statutory offences over common law ones. In R v Hall (1891) 1 QB 747 the court held that where a statute creates (or recreates) a duty and prescribes a particular penalty for a willful neglect of that duty the remedy by indictment is excluded.

In R v Rimmington, R v Goldstein (2005) UKHL63 at paragraph 30 the House of Lords confirmed this approach, saying:

'good practice and respect for the primacy of statute require that conduct falling within the terms of a specific statutory provision should be prosecuted under that provision unless there is good reason for doing otherwise.'

The use of the common law offence should therefore be limited to the following situations:

Where there is no relevant statutory offence, but the behaviour or the circumstances are such that they should nevertheless be treated as criminal;

Where there is a statutory offence but it would be difficult or inappropriate to use it. This might arise because of evidential difficulties in proving the statutory offence in the particular circumstances; because the maximum sentence for the statutory offence would be entirely insufficient for the seriousness of the misconduct.

Definition of the offence

The elements of the offence are summarised in Attorney General's Reference No 3 of 2003 (2004) EWCA Crim 868. The offence is committed when:

a public officer acting as such willfully neglects to perform his duty and/or willfully misconducts himself to such a degree as to amount to an abuse of the public's trust in the office holder without reasonable excuse or justification

The prosecution must have evidence to show that the suspect is a 'public officer'. There is no simple definition and each case must be assessed individually, taking into account the nature of the role, the duties carried out and the level of public trust involved.

The courts have been reluctant to provide a detailed definition of a public officer. The case-law contains an element of circularity, in that the cases tend to define a public officer as a person who carries out a public duty or has an office of trust. What may constitute a public duty or an office of trust must therefore be inferred from the facts of particular cases.

The judgment of Lord Mansfield in R v Bembridge (1783) 3 Doug KB 32 refers to a public officer having:

' an office of trust concerning the public, especially if attended with profit ... by whomever and in whatever way the officer is appointed'.

It does not seem that the person concerned must be the holder of an 'office' in a narrow or technical sense. The authorities suggest that it is the nature of the duties and the level of public trust involved that are relevant, rather than the manner or nature of appointment.

In R v Whitaker (1914) KB 1283 the court said:

'A public office holder is an officer who discharges any duty in the discharge of which the public are interested, more clearly so if he is paid out of a fund provided by the public.'

This approach was followed in a series of cases from other common law jurisdictions: R v Williams (1986) 39 WIR 129; R v Sacks (1943) SALR 413; R v Boston (1923) 33 CLR 386.

In R v Dytham (1979) 1 QB 723 Lord Widgery CJ talked of 'a public officer who has an obligation to perform a duty'.

Remuneration is a significant factor, but not an essential element. In R v Belton (2010) WLR (D) 283 the defendant was an unpaid voluntary member of the Independent Monitoring Board. The Court of Appeal held that remuneration was not an indispensable requirement for the holding of a public office, or for liability to prosecution for the offence of misconduct in a public office.

The fact that an individual was a volunteer might have a bearing on whether there had been willful misconduct, but was only indicative rather than determinative of whether an individual held a public office.

The court in Attorney General's Reference No 3 of 2003 (2004) EWCA Crim 868 referred to the unfairness that could arise where people who carry out similar duties may or may not be liable to prosecution depending on whether they can be defined as 'public officers'. What were once purely public functions are now frequently carried out by employees in private employment. An example is the role of the court security officer.

The court declined to define a public officer, however, but said:

'This potential unfairness adds weight, in our view, to the conclusion that the offence should be strictly confined but we do not propose to develop the point or to consider further the question of what, for present purposes, constitutes a public office.'

The following have been accepted as holding a public office by the courts over several centuries:

Coroner (1675) R v Parker 2 Lev 140
Constable (1703) R v Wyatt 1 Salk 380
Accountant in the office of the Paymaster General (1783) R v Bembridge 3 Doug K.B. 32
Justice of the Peace (1791) R v Sainsbury 4 T.R 451
Executive or ministerial officer (1819) R v Friar 1 Chit.Rep (KB) 702
Gaoler (1827) R v Cope 6 A%E 226
Mayor or burgess (1828) Henly v Mayor of Lyme 5 Bing 91
Overseer of the poor (1891) R v Hall 1 QB 747
Army officer (1914) R v Whitaker 10 Cr.App.R.245
County Court registrar (district judge) (1968) R v Llewellyn-Jones 1 Q.B.429
Police officer (1979) R v Dytham 69 Cr.App.R.387
Council maintenance officer (1995) R v Bowden 4 All E.R 505
Local councillor (2004) R v Speechley (2004) EWCA Crim 3067
Member of the Independent Monitoring Board for prisons (2010) R v Belton R v Belton (2010) EWCA Crim 2857

This list is illustrative only of the roles or functions that have been accepted by the courts over the years as falling within the definition of public officer. Each case must be taken on its own facts. The comments of the Court of Appeal in Attorney General's Reference No 3 of 2003 (2004) EWCA Crim 868 must be borne in mind concerning potential unfairness. The court took into account the fact that public functions are now frequently carried out by employees in private employment, for example those concerned with security at courts and the transport of defendants. There was the potential for unfairness if those holding a public office, such as police officers, were to be liable to a sanction not applicable to those in private employment who do similar work.

It is extremely difficult to extract from the cases any general identifying features of public officers in a contemporary context. A person may fall within the meaning of a public officer where one or more of the following characteristics applies to a role or function that they exercise with respect to the public at large:

Judicial or quasi-judicial.......

......Regulatory........Punitive.......Coercive......Investigative......

Representative (of the public at large)........Responsibility for public funds

Acting as such

The suspect must not only be a 'public officer'; the misconduct must also occur when acting in that capacity.

It is not sufficient that the person is a public officer and has engaged in some form of misconduct. The mere fact that a person is carrying out general duties as a public officer at the time of the alleged misconduct does not mean he or she is necessarily acting as a public officer in respect of the misconduct.

There must be a direct link between the misconduct and an abuse, misuse or breach of the specific powers and duties of the office or position.

The offence would also not normally apply to the actions of a public officer outside that role, unless the misconduct involved improper use of the public officer's specific powers or duties arising from the public office.

A deliberate misuse by an off-duty police officer of the powers of a constable, for example, may mean that the officer is 'acting as such' by virtue of his or her assumption of the powers of the office. Such a situation might arise if an off-duty police officer arrested an innocent man with whom he had a personal dispute or took steps in order to prevent or frustrate an enquiry.

The principles involved apply equally to holders of all public offices. In the case of a school governor or a local authority official or other such member of a public body, for example, it will be necessary to show that the misconduct was closely connected with exercising (or failing to exercise) the relevant public function.

Willful neglect or misconduct

Nature of the neglect or misconduct

The willful neglect or misconduct can be the result of a positive act or a failure to act. In the case of R v Dytham (1979) QB 722, for example, a police officer was held to have been correctly convicted when he made no move to intervene during a disturbance in which a man was kicked to death.

There must also be an element of knowledge or at least recklessness about the way in which the duty is carried out or neglected. The test is a subjective one and the public officer must be aware that his/her behaviour is capable of being misconduct.

Meaning of 'willful'

In Attorney General's Reference No 3 of 2003 the court approved the definition of 'willful' as 'deliberately doing something which is wrong knowing it to be wrong or with reckless indifference as to whether it is wrong or not'.

In R v G (2003) UK HL 50 Lord Bingham said with respect to inadvertence:

It is clearly blameworthy to take an obvious and significant risk of causing injury to another. But it is not clearly blameworthy to do something involving a risk of injury to another if one genuinely does not perceive the risk. Such a person may fairly be accused of stupidity or lack of imagination, but neither of those failings should expose him to conviction of serious crime or the risk of punishment.

Lord Steyn added:

the stronger the objective indications of risk, the more difficult it will be for defendants to repel the conclusion that they must have known. (R v G (2003) UK HL 50)

Abuse of the public's trust

Public officers carry out their duties for the benefit of the public as a whole. If they neglect or misconduct themselves in the course of those duties this may lead to a breach or abuse of the public's trust.

Seriousness of the neglect or misconduct

The behaviour must be serious enough to amount to an abuse of the public's trust in the office holder. In R v Dytham, Lord Widgery said that the element of culpability:

must be of such a degree that the misconduct impugned is

calculated to injure the public interest so as to call for condemnation and punishment.

In Attorney General's Reference No 3 of 2003 the court said that the misconduct must amount to:

"...an affront to the standing of the public office held. The threshold is a high one requiring conduct so far below acceptable standards as to amount to an abuse of the public's trust in the office holder".

Consequences

The likely consequences of any willful neglect or misconduct are relevant when deciding whether the conduct falls below the standard expected:

"It will normally be necessary to consider the likely consequences of the breach in deciding whether the conduct falls so far below the standard of conduct to be expected of the officer as to constitute the offence. The conduct cannot be considered in a vacuum: the consequences likely to follow from it, viewed subjectively ...will often influence the decision as to whether the conduct amounted to an abuse of the public's trust in the officer". (Attorney General's Reference No 3 of 2003).

Whilst there is no need to prove any particular consequences flowing from the misconduct, it must be proved that the defendant was reckless not just as to the legality of his behaviour, but also as to its likely consequences.

The consequences must be likely ones, as viewed subjectively by the defendant. Although the authorities do not say so, likely can probably be taken to mean at the very least 'reasonably foreseeable'; it is arguable that likely may mean 'probable' in this context.

Motive

In order to establish whether the behaviour is sufficiently serious to amount to the offence, the officer's motive is also relevant:

"...the question has always been, not whether the act done might, upon full and mature investigation, be found strictly right, but from what motive it had proceeded; whether from a dishonest, oppressive, or corrupt motive, under which description, fear and favour may generally be included, or from mistake or error..."

"To punish as a criminal any person who, in the gratuitous exercise of a public trust, may have fallen into error or mistake belongs only to the despotic ruler of an enslaved people, and is wholly abhorrent from the jurisprudence of this kingdom".

(R v Borron (1820) 3 B&Ald 432: Abbott CJ, at page 434.)

At its highest the motive may be malice or bad faith but they are not prerequisites. Reckless indifference would be sufficient

Without reasonable excuse or justification

It is not necessary for the prosecution to prove the absence of a reasonable excuse or justification, although the nature of the prosecution evidence should in practice negate any such element.

The defendant may advance evidence of a reasonable excuse or justification. It is for the jury to determine whether the evidence reveals the necessary culpability.

Charging Practice

General principles

Where there is clear evidence of one or more statutory offences, they should usually form the basis of the case, provided the offences give the court adequate sentencing powers. The 'public office' element can be put forward as an aggravating factor for sentencing purposes.

A comparison may be made with charges of perverting the course of justice. In R v Sookoo (2002) EWCA Crim 800 the Court of Appeal held that adding a charge of attempting to pervert the course of justice along with counts for the principal offence or offences was only appropriate where a case had serious aggravating features (such as wasted police time and resources or detention of members of the public following false implication of them in the offence by the accused).

Similar reasoning should apply to the charging of misconduct in public office. When charging such an offence the prosecutor should provide a detailed review note of the reasons for doing so in the particular case. The note should make reference to any relevant factors referred to in this guidance, particularly where a statutory offence covering the behaviour in question is either charged or could have been charged.

For example an assault by a police officer committed on duty should not automatically be considered as misconduct in public office. A charge of assault would normally provide the court with adequate sentencing powers and the ability to take into account the breach of trust by the officer as an aggravating factor. See R v Dunn (2003) 2 Cr.App.R.(S).

Similarly, prosecutions for unauthorised access to or use of computer or other data systems should normally be conducted using the specific offence provided in section 55 Data Protection Act 1998. Only where the circumstances are such that a fine would not be an appropriate or sufficient penalty should a prosecution for misconduct in public office be considered.

Misconduct in public office should be considered only where:

there is no suitable statutory offence for a piece of serious misconduct (such as a serious breach of or neglect of a public duty that is not in itself a criminal offence);

there was serious misconduct or a deliberate failure to perform a duty owed to the public, with serious potential or actual consequences for the public;

the facts are so serious that the court's sentencing powers would otherwise be inadequate

Level of misconduct required

The offence is, in essence, one of abuse of the power or responsibilities of the office held.

Misconduct in public office should be used for serious examples of misconduct when there is no appropriate statutory offence that would adequately describe the nature of the misconduct or give the court adequate sentencing powers.

The third element of the definition of the offence provides an important test when deciding whether to proceed with an offence of misconduct in public office. Unless the misconduct in question amounts to such an abuse of trust, a prosecution for misconduct in public office should not be considered.

The culpability 'must be of such a degree that the misconduct impugned is calculated to injure the public interest so as to call for condemnation and punishment' (R v Dytham 1979 QB 722).

The fact that a public officer has acted in a way that is in breach of his or her duties, or which might expose him/her to disciplinary proceedings, is not in itself enough to constitute the offence.

Examples of behaviour that have in the past fallen within the offence include:

willful excesses of official authority;

'malicious' exercises of official authority;

willful neglect of a public duty;

intentional infliction of bodily harm, imprisonment, or other injury upon a person; frauds and deceits.

Breaches of duty

Some of the most difficult cases involve breaches of public duty that do not involve dishonesty or corruption.

In all cases, however, the following matters should be addressed:

Was there a breach of a duty owed to the public (not merely an employment duty or a general duty of care)?

Was the breach more than merely negligent or attributable to incompetence or a mistake (even a serious one)?

Did the defendant have a subjective awareness of a duty to act or subjective recklessness as to the existence of a duty?

Did the defendant have a subjective awareness that the action or omission might be unlawful?

Did the defendant have a subjective awareness of the likely consequences of the action or omission.

Did the officer realise (subjective test) that there was a risk not only that his or her conduct was unlawful but also a risk that the consequences of that behaviour would occur?

Were those consequences 'likely' as viewed subjectively by the defendant? Did the officer realise that those consequences were 'likely' and yet went on to take the risk?

Regard must be had to motive.

Dishonesty or corruption

Dishonesty or corrupt behaviour are not essential elements of the offence of misconduct in public office.

If, however, an allegation of misconduct in public office arises from circumstances involving the acquisition of property by theft or fraud, or where the holder of a public office is alleged to have made improper claims for public funds in circumstances said to be criminal, an essential ingredient of the offence is proof that the defendant was dishonest.

In R v W (2010) EWCA 372, a police officer used an official credit card for personal purchases. The Court of Appeal held that an essential ingredient of the offence of misconduct in public office in such circumstances was that the defendant was dishonest, and had not merely flagrantly broken the rules governing the use of the card.

When the allegation does involve the acquisition of property by theft or fraud, any misconduct should normally be prosecuted using appropriate statutory offences on the basis that an appropriate statutory offence should always be used where available in accordance with R v Rimmington, R v Goldstein (2005) UKHL63. (See Policy above). The fact that the offence was committed in the course of a public office is an aggravating element.

Regina v Bowden Court of Appeal (Criminal Division) (Lord Justice Hirst, Mr Justice Hidden and Mr Justice Mitchell) 24 February 1995
The common law offence of misconduct in public office is not limited to officers or agents of the Crown but applies also to local authority employees.

The Court of Appeal dismissed the appellant's appeal against conviction of misconduct in a public office.

The appellant was employed by the Stoke-on-Trent City Council as the miscellaneous maintenance manager of the city works department, the council's direct labour organisation. He was convicted of dishonestly causing, when a holder of public office, work to be carried out at premises when those works were not required under the council's policy. The premises were let to the appellant's lady friend.

CONDUCT PROSECUTED AS MISCONDUCT IN PUBLIC OFFICE
Conduct that can only be prosecuted as misconduct in public office
(1) Public office holders who exploit their positions to facilitate a sexual relationship
(2) Public office holders who use their positions to facilitate a personal relationship which may create a conflict with the proper performance of the functions of their position
(3) Public office holders who deliberately act in a prejudicial or biased manner or under a conflict of interest
(4) Neglect of duty by public office holders which results in serious consequences, or a risk of serious consequences arising
(5) Public office holders who fail properly to protect information that comes into their possession by virtue of their positions

Conduct that is prosecuted as misconduct in public office but could be prosecuted as an alternative criminal offence

(1) Public office holders who exploit their positions to facilitate financial gain
(2) Payments made or received in advance of an individual becoming a public office holder
(3) Interference with evidence
(4) The conveyance of non-prohibited, but potentially harmful or disruptive, articles into prison
(5) Public office holders who fail properly to protect information that comes into their possession by virtue of their positions

EXCLUDING THE PRESS AND PUBLIC

The Council's legal obligations under the Public Bodies(Admission to Meetings) Act 1960. The act provides

"1 Admission of public to meetings of local authorities and other bodies.

(1)   Subject to subsection(2) below, any meeting of a body exercising public functions being a body to which this Act applies shall be open to the public.

(2) A body may, by resolution , exclude the public from a meeting (whether during the whole or part of the proceedings) whenever publicity would be prejudicial to the public interest by reason of the confidential nature of the business to be transacted or for other special reasons stated in the resolution and arising from the nature of the business or of the proceedings; and where such a resolution is passed, this Act shall not require the meeting to be open to the public during proceedings to which this resolution applies."

The wording of the legislation the "none specific wording" used in standard exclusion of the press and public from Town Council meetings " by reason of the confidential nature of the business" fully satisfies the legal requirements.

The Town Council is not governed by the Local Government (Access to Information) Act 1985 and more particularly Schedule 12A thereof ...and are not legally obliged to provide the public with "specific reasons" for the exclusion of the press and public either by the governing legislation or under the Freedom of Information Act.That said, **when deciding whether or not to exclude the press and public from meetings, the Proper Officer, should have specific regard to the advice on this matter as set out in the leading text "Local Council Administration" by Charles Arnold Baker,** this text, which specifically covers the law as it applies to Town and Parish Councils, states at page 60, Eighth Edition, published by LexisNexis

"In few cases is there any good reason for excluding the press or the public from meetings.....As a rule, however, it is desirable to treat the discussion of the following types of business as confidential:

(a) **Engagement, terms of service, conduct and dismissal of employees;**
(b) **Terms of tenders, proposals and counter-proposals in negotiation for contracts**
(c) **Preparation of cases in legal proceedings; and**
(d) **The early stages of any dispute"**

At no time should this ever be used just to try and cover up something which is Administratively or Politically embarrassing. The Press and Public have recourse to law if the reason for excluding is not valid.

The public interest test

The public interest test requires that information should be withheld under an exemption if, in all the circumstances of the case, the public interest in maintaining the exemption outweighs the public interest in disclosing the information. Where the balance is seen as equal the information must be released. In all cases, the decision to release or withhold will be a matter of judgement at the time of the request. The decisions should be recorded, documenting the reasons on both sides as objectively as possible, to make the decision and to be able to account for reasons. Some points to consider when assessing the public interest:

Factors In Favour Of Disclosure

Whether it would promote accessibility to information, promoting transparency and accountability.
Whether a document would disclose reasons for a decision made on behalf of the public and/or enable them to challenge these decisions.
Whether disclosure would contribute to a public debate on a matter of public interest.
Whether disclosure would enhance scrutiny and thereby improve accountability and participation.
Whether disclosure would bring to light important matters of public health and safety.
This list is not exhaustive, and in all cases proper consideration should be given over whether to disclose or withhold information. The public interest does not include the protection of individuals, in their capacity as officers of the Council, or Councillors from embarrassment.

The Information Commissioners Office (ICO) will certainly rule on any issue around disclosure.

And now for something completely different !

Some useful quotes I have collected over the last 45 years

1.   "Serve the public trust"
2.   "Protect the innocent"
3.   "Uphold the law"

You shall not side with the great against the powerless

Let right be done, no matter what the cost

A brave man's wounds are seldom on his back.

A clear conscience fears not false accusations.

Adversity makes a man wise, not rich.

A few honest men are better than numbers:

A fool always finds a greater fool to admire him:

A fool believes everything.

A fool must now and then be right by chance.

A guilty conscience needs no accuser.

"Always do right. This will gratify some people and astonish the rest.' —Mark Twain

A liar should have a good memory.

A man will never change his mind - if he has no mind to change.

A noisy man is always in the right.

A person who talks about his inferiors hasn't any:

A well timed silence hath more eloquence than speech.

A wise man does not accept people on their words alone.

A wise man never knows all; only fools know everything.

A wise man does not reject a man's suggestions simply because he does not like the man who is making them.

Advice is seldom welcome, and those who need it the most always like it the least:

Advice when most needed, is least heeded.

After all that's said and done, a lot more is said than done.

All knowledge is of itself of some value.
Always be ready to speak your mind, and a base man will avoid you:

An expert is one who knows more and more about less and less.

An idea isn't responsible for the people who believe in it.

An idealist is one who on noticing that a rose smells better than a cabbage; concludes that it will also make a better soup.

An occasion lost can never be redeemed.

Anger restrained is wisdom gained.

Any fool can criticise, condemn and complain - and most fools do:

Anything is possible if you don't know what you're talking about.

Assumption is the mother of all screw-ups.

Be more concerned with your character than with your reputation. Your character is what you really are while your reputation is merely what others think you are.

Behind every argument is someone's ignorance.

Believe no tales from an enemy's tongue.

Believe those who are seeking the truth. Doubt those who find it.

Better a lie that heals than a truth that wounds.

Better an open enemy, than a false friend.

Better to ask the way than go astray.

Beware that you do not lose the substance by grasping at the shadow.

Blessed is he that expects nothing for he shall never be disappointed.

Blessed is the man who, having nothing to say, abstains from giving evidence of the fact.

By itself, truth always wins. A lie always needs an accomplice:

Character is always lost when a high ideal is sacrificed on the altar of conformity and popularity .

Crank: a man with a new idea, until it succeeds.

Defeat is for those who acknowledge it.

Do not forget little kindnesses and do not remember small faults.

Do not then be afraid of defeat – for you are never so near victory as when defeated in a good cause.

Do right and fear no man.

Do what you feel in your heart to be right - for you'll be criticized anyway. You'll be damned if you do, and damned if you don't.

Don't be deterred in the fanatical application of your sterile logic:

Don't go near the water until you learn to swim.

Doubt is the key of knowledge.

Error of opinion should be tolerated where reason is left free to combat it:

Even a naturally good man, if you slander his character, will often show himself towards you as bad as you have painted him.

Even the wisest of the wise may err.

Every normal man must be tempted, at times, to spit on his hands, hoist the black flag, and begin slitting throats.

Every oak was once an acorn.

Every why has a wherefore.

Every time we open our mouths, people can look into our minds.

Everything comes down to this - to win or lose, one never stays motionless. Because to stop moving is to begin losing.

Everything that exceeds the bounds of moderation - has an unstable foundation.

Example is the school of mankind, and they will learn at no other.

Experience - the name men give to their mistakes.

Experience is the mother of wisdom.

Eyes will not see when the heart wishes to be blind, desire always conceals truth:

Facts do not cease to exist because they are ignored:

Facts that are not frankly faced, have a habit of stabbing us in the back:
Faultfinders ought to live straight and walk straight, before they set about instructing others.

Fools bite one another, but wise men agree together.

Fortune favours those who use their judgement.

From the sublime to the ridiculous there is only one step.

Progress is not an accident, but a necessity - it is part of nature.

Genius does what it must, and talent does what it can.

Gratitude preserves old friendships, and procures new.

Haste is the sister of repentance.

He who aims at the moon may hit the top of a tree; he who aims at the top of a tree is unlikely to get off the ground.

He is unworthy to live who lives only for himself.

He begins to die that quits his desires.

He can compress the most words into the smallest ideas of anyone I know:

He can who believes he can.

He conquers who endures.

He has but one principle, that of self-interest, the desire to insult.

He belongs to the school of lying, hypocrisy and cowardice:

He has made his conscience not his guide but his accomplice:

He has set his heart on being a martyr, and I have set mine on disappointing him.

He is a self-made man and worships his creator.

He is lifeless that is faultless.

He makes no friend who never made a foe.

He that commits a fault, thinks everyone speaks of it.

He that always gives way to others will end in having no principles of his own

He that does ill. Hates the light.

He that is down need fear no fall.

He that forgives, gains the victory.

He that is afraid to throw the dice, will never throw a six.

He that is born a fool is never cured.

He that is master of himself, will soon be master of others.

He that knows nothing doubts nothing.

He that will not apply new remedies must expect new evils; for time is the greatest innovator.

He that will not be counselled. Cannot be helped.

He thinks the whole worlds against him. It's the only thing he and the world see eye to eye on:

He who is firm and resolute in will, moulds the world to himself.

He who knows nothing is confident of everything:

He who permits himself to be insulted deserves the insult:

He's always talking about his inferiors, but no one has ever been able to find them:

Hope is a good breakfast, but it is a bad supper.

How like sheep some people are.

Human progress has often depended on the courage of a man who dared to be different.
I have never made but one prayer to God, a very short one; " O lord, make my enemies ridiculous." and God granted it.

I never attribute to malice that which is adequately explained by stupidity.

I beseech you in the bowels of Christ; think it possible you may be mistaken.

I accept failure only as a step on the path to success.

I am an idealist, I don't know where I am going, but I'm on my way.

The only thing that can keep growing without nourishment is an ego.

The weaker the argument the stronger the words.

I am only one, but I am one, I cannot do everything, but I can do something, what I can do, I ought to do, and what I ought to do, by the grace of God I will do.

I Have found some of the best reasons I ever had for remaining at the bottom simply by looking at the men at the top.

I have found Holmes methodology of deductive reasoning quite useful:
when you have eliminated the impossible, whatever remains, however improbable, must be the truth.

I have never met a man who has given me as much trouble as myself:

I read somewhere that human intelligence is reckoned to be half a million years old. Listening to him you'd think it was still at the nappy stage:

I think that, bearing in mind, and after due consideration, and considering all the implications and points of view, there appears to have been a development which could precipitate a re-appraisal of our position:

I think the purpose of life is to be useful, to be responsible, to be honorable, to be compassionate. It is, after all, to matter: to count, to stand for something, to have made some difference that you lived at all.

I will have nothing to do with a man who can blow hot and cold with the same breath.

I wish I was as sure about anything as he is about everything:
Ideas are often poor ghosts, but sometimes they are made of flesh:

If I Spent as much time doing the things I worry about getting done as I do worrying then I wouldn't have anything to worry about:

"If it doesn't feel right, don't do it. That is the lesson, and that lesson alone will save you a lot of grief."

If a man hope not, he shall not find that which he did not hope, that is beyond search and reaching.

If it has to choose who will be crucified, the crowd will always save Barabbas.

If you can't run things your own way, you can always say a little later: " I Told you so."

If a man will begin with certainties, he shall end in doubts, but if he will be content to begin with doubts, he shall end in certainties.

If it were not for hope, the heart would break.
If only you'd use your brains a little bit more you could honestly call yourself a half wit:

If you can't ride two horses at once, you shouldn't be in the circus.

If you do something which you are sure will meet with everybody's approval, somebody won't like it.

If you don't fight for what you want in life, you will never achieve it.

If you don't think about problems that might come, before they actually appear, you will not be able to solve them when they do appear.

If you explain so clearly that nobody can miss-understand, somebody will.

If you think you are beaten, you are, if you think you dare not, you don't, if you'd like to win, but think you can't, it's almost a cinch you won't.

If you want to find out what is wrong with a man, elect him to public office.

If you will not fight for right when you can easily win without bloodshed; if you will not fight when your victory is sure and not too costly; you may come to the moment when you will have to fight with all the odds against you and only a precarious chance of survival. There may even be a worse case. You may have to fight when there is no hope of victory, because it is better to perish than to live as slaves.   -Winston Churchill

In matters of progress, it's not where we stand but which direction we are moving.

In an organisation in which men have to accept, outwardly at least, some obviously absurd doctrine, the best men must either become stupid or disaffected.

In matters of progress it's not where we stand but which direction we are headed.

In ordinary life it is rare indeed for people to form their beliefs by a process of logical deduction from facts ascertained by a rigorous search for all available evidence and a judicious assessment of its probative value. In greater or in less degree according to their temperaments, their training, their intelligence, they are swayed by prejudice, rely on intuition instead of reasoning, leap to conclusions on inadequate evidence and fail to recognise the cogency of material which might cast doubt on the validity of the conclusions they reach. But despite the imperfection of the mental process by which the belief is arrived at it may still be 'honest', that is, a positive belief that the conclusions they have reached are true.

Intellect is invisible to the man who has none:

Is a man who takes more words than necessary to tell more than he knows.

It is an event upon which it is difficult to speak, and impossible to remain silent.

It is not every question that deserves an answer.

It is always the season for the old to learn.

It is as hard to follow good advice as to give it.

It is bad enough that so many people believe things without any evidence. What is worse is that some people have no conception of evidence and regard facts as just someone else's opinion.

It is better to do well than say well.

It is impossible to defeat an ignorant man in an argument.

It is just as well that justice is blind, she might not like some of the things done in her name if she could see them.

It is only among fools that the wise are judged to be destitute of wisdom.

It is still one of the tragedies of human history. That the " children of darkness " are frequently more determined and zealous than the " children of the light."

It is the unknown that defines our existence.

It is wiser to find out than suppose.

It isn't necessary or perhaps even good to have everyone like you. That idea in politics can make you the worst kind of person. You will be spineless, uninteresting, lacking in character. One should measure a person by looking at the enemies he has made.

It's all the young can do for the old, to shock them and keep them up to date.

It's alright to have an open mind, if you know what to let in.

It's more democratic to do things secretly.

It's more expensive to do things cheaply.

Jesus said: " and if the blind lead the blind. Both shall fall into the ditch."

Kindness is the noblest weapon to conquer with.

Let he that would move the world, first move himself:

Let thy speech be better than silence, or be silent

Liars ought to have good memories:

Life is half spent before we know what it is.

Life is short and time is swift.

Long absence changes a friend.

Luck and temper rule the world:

Man's fear of ideas is probably the greatest dyke holding back human knowledge and happiness:

Many highly intelligent people are caught in the intelligence trap: They take a position on a subject and then use their thinking ability solely to support that position. The more able they are to support the position, the less do they see any need to actually explore the subject —so they become trapped in one point of view.

Many people who meet with misfortune through their own fault, put the blame on others.

Many so-called open minds should be closed for repairs.

Men are blind in their own cause.

Men at some time are masters of their fates, the fault dear Brutus, is not in our stars, but in ourselves.

Misfortunes find their way even on the darkest night. Good advice has no price.

Most people in fact. Will not take the trouble in finding out the truth, but are much more inclined to accept the first story they hear.

Most of us know how to say nothing, few of us know when.

Most of us know how to say nothing, few of us know when:

Most every argument is closely reasoned   some are merely formal, some commonsense and some almost flippant:

Nature has given us two ears, two eyes and only one tongue; therefore we should hear and see more than we speak.

Nature didn't make us perfect, so she did the next best thing, she made us blind to our faults.

Never create a problem for which you do not have the answer.

"Never doubt that a small group of thoughtful, committed citizens can change the world. Indeed, it is the only thing that ever has."

Never judge from appearances.

Never lie to someone who trusts you, and never trust someone who lies.
Never trust a man with short legs, brains too near their bottoms:

No bird soars too high, if he soars with his own wings:
No idea becomes reality without sacrifice.

No man is the worse for knowing himself.

None of your past experiences has prepared you for this consequence.

No one was ever ruined by speaking the truth.

No tie can oblige the perfidious.

Not every argument is closely reasoned - some are merely formal, some common-sense, and some almost flippant.

Nothing is impossible for the person who doesn't have to do it himself.
Nothing great was ever achieved without enthusiasm.

Nothing is certain but the unforeseen.

Nothing is ever a failure; it can always serve as a negative example.

Nothing is given so freely as advice

Nothing will ever be attempted if all possible objections must be overcome first.

Nothing worthwhile is easy.

Oaths are but words, and words are but wind.

Observe thyself as thy greatest enemy would do, so thou shalt be thy greatest friend.

"Of all tyrannies, a tyranny sincerely exercised for the good of its victims may be the most oppressive. It would be better to live under robber barons than under omnipotent moral busybodies... those who torment us for our own good will torment us without end, for they do so with the approval of their own conscience." (C S Lewis)Old men dream dreams, young men see visions:

One can defeat extremists despite their massive expenditure of lung power.

One gives nothing so freely as advice:

One of the greatest pains to human nature, is the pain of a new idea.

Only people who do things get criticised.

Opportunity - not only strike while the iron is hot, but make it hot by striking:

Oratory is the of making deep sounds from the chest seem like important of messages from the brain:

Our grand business is not to see what lies dimly in the distance, but to do what lies clearly to hand.

People who attempt things without due consideration suffer for it and get laughed at into the bargain.

People who talk to you about others behind their back, will usually do the same with you.

People prefer to wrong together with their friends, than right, in the company of their opponents.

People tend to make rules for others and exceptions for themselves.

Pick battles big enough to matter, small enough to win

Piss not against the wind.

Politics is the only profession for which no preparation is thought necessary:

Politics is almost as exciting as war but more dangerous, in war you can be killed only once, in politics many times.

Really honest people are seldom impressed by their own ability.

Reason is superior to authority.

Remember, that even the feeblest man, if you trample him in the mud, can find a way, someday, to pay you back.

Ridicule is the first and last argument of fools.

Scientists say we are what we eat, nuts must be a commoner diet than we had thought.

Seek that which may be found.

Silence is the virtue of fools.

Silence: what would follow if the average politician spoke his mind:

So shines a good deed in a weary world.

Some people talk simply because they think sound is more manageable than silence:
Some fool, long ago, probably a roman said that to know how to command., a man must first learn to obey. This is the opposite of the truth: the man that has learnt to obey will either have lost all personal initiative or will have become so filled with rage against the authorities that his initiative will have become destructive and cruel.

Some people are indebted to their imagination for their facts.

Some people talk simply because they find sound more manageable than silence:
Some people have nothing to say, but you have to listen a long time to find out:

Some people have tact, others tell the truth:

Sometimes we must persevere along our chosen course. No matter how many and depressing the setbacks-no ideal becomes reality without sacrifice.

Statistics are no substitute for judgement:
Take away the cause and the effect must cease.
The absent are always in the wrong.

The absent party is always to blame.

The first three rules of any bureaucracy are:

1) that it is always looking for ways to extend its powers;
2) everything it does is for a socially desirable reason, even if it serves no useful purpose; and
3) however many mistakes it makes, it is always right. But the fourth rule of bureaucracy is that, when officials claim to be "consulting", they end up doing just what they proposed to do in the first place.

The man who adequately understands his own circumstances will act wisely, and will even be happy in the face of what to another would be misfortune.

The only people who find what they are looking for in life are the faultfinders.

The person who goes through life looking for something soft will find it between his ears.

The person with a mind that is too open gets a lot of worthless ideas dumped into it.

The power which resides in him is new in nature and none but he knows what that is which he can do, nor does he know until he has tried.

The reason why some of them find it difficult to think, is that they haven't had any experience:

The right to be heard, does not automatically include the right to be taken seriously.

The best tranquilizer is a clear conscience.

The brave may fall but cannot yield.

The first blow, is half the battle.

The first step is the hardest.

The laws of humanity supersede those of any state.

The louder the argument the smaller the prospect of compromise.

The measure of a man's life, is the well spending of it, and not the length.

The minute he gets up to speak, some fool always begins to talk.

The only sure thing about luck is that it will change:

The only thing necessary for the triumph of evil is for good men to do nothing.

The only thing that can keep growing without nourishment is an ego.

The person who has the approval of his conscience has a powerful ally.

The person who says there's nothing new in the world might try thinking,

The price of liberty is eternal vigilance.

The recipe for perpetual ignorance is: be satisfied with your opinions and content with your knowledge.

The right honourable gentleman is indebted to his imagination for his facts:

The strongest man on earth, is he who stands most alone.

The submitting to one wrong brings on another.

"The time is always right to do what is right." —Martin Luther King, The unexpected always happens.

The voice of the majority is no proof of justice.

The weaker the argument the stronger the words.

The wind in one's face makes one wise.

The wise man thinks about his troubles only when there is some purpose in doing so - at other times he thinks about other things, or if it is night about nothing at all.

There are many good people who hold sincere and passionate views,   but it is not enough to be good and sincere.

There are no hopeless situations, there are only people who take hopeless attitudes.

There are those who speak because they have something to say, and those who speak because they have to say something:

There is no merit where there is no trial; till experience stamps the mark of strength, cowards pass for heroes, and faith for falsehood.

There is nothing so minute or inconsiderable that I would not rather know it than not.

There appears to have been a development which could precipitate a re-appraisal of our position:

There are implications, repercussions, reverberations, knock-on effects. We need time to sift and weigh evidence, examine the options, test arguments, review, research, and consult. We need lots of input, we don't want to make any announcements until we have examined every implication and ramification:

There are in nature neither rewards nor punishments - there are consequences:

There are so few who can grow old with a good grace:

There is a time in every man's education in life when he arrives at the conclusion or conviction that envy is ignorance, that imitation is suicide, that he must take himself for better, for worse, that though the wide universe is full of good - nothing comes to him but through his effort bestowed on that plot of ground which is given to him to till.

There is always room at the top.

There is nothing so small that it can't be blown out of all proportion.

They never open their mouth without subtracting from the sum of human knowledge:

They take a position on a subject and then use their thinking ability solely to support that position.

Those who plot against their friends, often find to their surprise that they destroy themselves into the bargain.

Those who make peaceful revolution impossible, will make violent revolution inevitable:
Those who sit quietly and do nothing

Those who stand for nothing fall for anything.

Those who talk about doing things

Those who talk about sitting quietly and doing nothing

Though the sword of justice is sharp, it will not slay the innocent.

Time and tide wait for no man.
Time lost cannot be recalled.

To avoid criticism, do nothing, say nothing, be nothing.

To some, if the facts do not conform to the theory, they must be disposed of.

To be criticised is not necessarily to be wrong.

To be out of harmony with one's surroundings is, of course, a misfortune; but it is not always a misfortune to be avoided at all costs. Where the environment is stupid or cruel or prejudiced, it is a sign of merit to be out of harmony with it.
To become what we are capable of becoming is the only end in life:

To deceive oneself is easy.

To see what is right and not to do it, is want of courage.

To the ordinary working man, the sort you would meet in any pub on Saturday night, socialism does not mean much more than better wages, shorter hours, and nobody bossing you about....... G. Orwell.

Trouble brings experience and experience brings wisdom.

Truth is rarely pure and never simple.

Truth fears no trial.

Two things a man should never be angry at: what he can help, and what he cannot help.

Unanimity is dangerous, and I fear nothing more than conformity.

Very often those who make this nation what it is, are not the ones who hit the headlines, but those who make them possible.

Violence in the voice is often only the death rattle of reason in the throat:

Virtue is not left to stand alone. He who practices it will have neighbours.

We wish to throw no one into the shade, but we demand our own place in the sun.

We go by the majority vote, and if the majority are insane, it the sane who must go to the asylum.

We learn wisdom by seeing the misfortunes of others.

We sometimes forget that if one follows one's self interest one wants to be safe, whereas the path of justice and honour involves one in danger and controversy - and where danger is concerned people as a rule are not very venturesome.

We soon believe what we desire.

What is possible is not invariably right. Equally. What is right is not always possible.

Whatever you do, you will encounter criticism. Someone will say, 'Why have you done this or said that? You should have made some other move instead.' So, is that a good enough reason to do nothing at all? Why, of course not. It is all the more reason to trust your deepest, most instinctive impulse and to let it lead you further down an important path. You may yet discover that the only way to attain meaningful progress is to contribute to a conflict that eventually causes everything to come out properly into the open.

When a man is determined to get his knife into someone, he will turn a deaf ear to any plea no matter how just.

When a man is wrong and won't admit it he always gets angry.

When a stupid person is doing something they are ashamed of, they always declares it is their duty:

When a thing is done. Advice comes too late.

When all is said and done, as a rule, more is said than done

When bad men combine, the good must associate, else they will fall, one by one, an unpitied sacrifice in a contemptible struggle.

When I hear somebody sigh, 'Life is hard,' I am always tempted to ask, 'Compared to what?'

When fortune smiles embrace her.

When looking for a reason why people do certain things, never rule out sheer stupidity.

When people profess to do what is impossible, the simplest test will often show them up for the imposters they are.

Where ignorance is bliss, tis folly to be wise.
Where there is whispering there is lying.

Who will not be ruled by the rudder, must be ruled by the rock.

Why do you sit there looking like an envelope without an address on it:

Wisdom is based on common sense and humility, not on winning arguments.

You have sat too long here for any good that you been doing, depart I say and let us have done with you, in the name of god go.

You cannot fight against the future, time is on our side.

Truth is on the march, nothing can stop it now.

Here I stand, I cannot do otherwise.

You can never cross the ocean unless you have the courage to lose sight of the shore.

You can't tell a book by its cover.

You have not converted a man because you have silenced him.

You may have genius, the contrary is, of course probable:

You may not have many faults but you certainly make the most of the ones you have:

You must be the reason for contraception:

You think me the child of my circumstances, I make my circumstances:

You'd think that such a little brain, would be lonely in such a big head:

Good character is more to be praised than outstanding talent. Most talents are, to some extent, a gift. Good character, by contrast, is not given to us. We have to build it piece by piece-by thought, choice, courage and determination.

That something happened to you is of no importance to anyone, not even to you. The important thing about you is what you choose to make happen—your values and choices. That which happened by accident—what family you were born into, in what country, and where you went to school—is totally unimportant.
I ask the question (is Cllr xxxxxxxx a bit stupid?) not to be gratuitously offensive, although I acknowledge it could be read in those terms, but in a genuine spirit of inquiry. If the man is not stupid, why does he repeatedly behave as though he is? For the leader of a political party, his grasp of politics seems quite limited. evasive, not at home to Mr Detail & devoid of ideas

Sir Humphrey Appleby

... NO THANK YOU
Please accept gratitudinal feedback regarding expressed proposal. After perusal of current operant limitations however, acceptance of aforementioned appears reluctantly contradicted.

....YOU MUST BE JOKING:
Inasmuch as the situation heretofore described fits unsuccessfully within a logical infrastructure and defies application of normative analysis and elucidation , the inevitable conclusion is that intent is facetious.

....WHAT :
Reiteration of the penultimate anomalous informational interchange would ameliorate potential non-comprehension and mis-directional expenditure of cognitive capacities in unorthodox proliferation of unintended dynamics

....THIS WON'T WORK:
There exists maximal negative implications in the unidirectional projection of this course of action which would result in the non-maturation of the concept and its premature termination.

....I DISAGREE:
Inherent flaws in the totality of determinative coherence of the foregoing statement lead to an inevitable polarisation of opinion resulting in divergent, if not contradictory, modes of mindset.

....THAT'S NOT TRUE:
Falsificatory and self -exclusional aspects of the qualitative accuracy of the foregoing's factual content contribute to its limited contextual veracity and resultant believability breakdown.

....GO TO HELL:
Substandard proficiency combined with your non co-operation displayed when apprised of aforesaid labour ineffectuality's make my sole recourse to accordingly recommend your instantaneous dispatch to an infernal destination.

I believe you have made an incorrect analysis of the facts at hand

Since your action did not produce the desired result, the only available solution would be to re-examine your decision making process and look for errors.

This is a very complex set of variables to co-ordinate.

"There is a time to let things happen, and a time to make things happen."

"A moment of choice is a moment of truth. It's the testing point of our character and competence."

"If you just set out to be liked, you would be prepared to compromise on anything at any time, and you would achieve nothing."

"You may be disappointed if you fail, but you are doomed if you don't try."

"It's not differences that divide us. It's our judgments about each other that do."

The ultimate measure of man is not where he stands in moments of comfort and convenience, but where he stands at times of challenge and controversy. —Dr. Martin Luther King Jr.

"Great leaders are almost always great simplifiers, who can cut through argument, debate, and doubt to offer a solution everybody can understand."

"I can honestly say that I was never affected by the question of the success of an undertaking. If I felt it was the right thing to do, I was for it regardless of the possible outcome."

"Better to fail at doing the right thing than to succeed at doing the wrong thing."

"It is not the strongest of the species that survive, nor the most intelligent, but the one most responsive to change." —Charles Darwin

One of the earliest proponents of the scientific method was Abu Ali Ibn al-Hassan Ibn al-Hussain Ibn al-Hussain Ibn al-Haytham, a mathematician, astronomer and philosopher of science in 11th-century Iraq, Al-Haytham held that —the seeker after truth – his beautiful phrase for the scientist – —does not place his faith in any mere consensus, however broad or venerable. Instead, said Al-Haytham, he checks and checks and checks again. —The road to the truth is long and hard, but that is the road we must follow.

Villains who twirl their moustaches are easy to spot, those who clothe themselves in good deeds are well camouflaged.

Conspiracy:
When a machination is real no one knows about it, and when it's suspected, it's almost never real, except in paranoid delusions for those who believe.

Sir Humphrey: Well Minister, if you ask me for a straight answer, then I shall say that, as far as we can see, looking at it by and large, taking one thing with another in terms of the average of departments, then in the final analysis it is probably true to say, that at the end of the day, in general terms, you would probably find that, not to put too fine a point on it, there probably wasn't very much in it one way or the other. As far as one can see, at this stage.

With the first link, the chain is forged, the first speech censured, the first thought forbidden, the first freedom denied,   chains us all irrevocably, the wisdom and warning, the first time any man's freedom is trodden on we are all damaged

INDEX

Printed in Great Britain
by Amazon

54872767R00149